THE
WAY
TO
INVE$T

Also by Ginita Wall

. . . .

The Way to Save

Our Money, Our Selves

Smart Ways to Save Money
During and After Divorce

THE
WAY
TO
INVE$T

· · · · · · · · · · · · · ·

A FIVE-STEP BLUEPRINT
FOR GROWING YOUR MONEY
THROUGH MUTUAL FUNDS, WITH
AS LITTLE AS $50 PER MONTH

Ginita Wall, CPA, CFP

An Owl Book
Henry Holt and Company
New York

Henry Holt and Company, Inc.
Publishers since 1866
115 West 18th Street
New York, New York 10011

Henry Holt® is a registered
trademark of Henry Holt and Company, Inc.

Published in Canada by Fitzhenry & Whiteside Ltd.,
195 Allstate Parkway, Markham, Ontario L3R 4T8.

Library of Congress Cataloging-in-Publication Data
Wall, Ginita.
   The way to invest: a five-step blueprint for growing your
money through mutual funds, with as little as $50 per month /
Ginita Wall. — 1st ed.
      p.   cm.
   "An Owl book."
   Includes index.
   1. Mutual funds.   2. Saving and investment.   I. Title.
HG4530.W27   1995   95-13327
332.63'27—dc20   CIP

ISBN 0-8050-3493-5

Henry Holt books are available for special promotions and premiums.
For details contact: Director, Special Markets.

First Edition—1995

Designed by Victoria Hartman

Printed in the United States of America
All first editions are printed on acid-free paper.∞

10   9   8   7   6   5   4   3   2   1

To my father,
who taught me to invest,
and in loving memory
of my mother,
who taught me to write,
and Hannah, my
patient five-book Muse.

CONTENTS

· · · · · · · ·

ACKNOWLEDGMENTS

Over the past eight years, many, many people contributed information that eventually became the book you are holding. Thanks especially to Candace Bahr, John Baranowski, and David Hirons, stockbrokers, who were patient sounding boards and a constant source of new ideas; to Victoria F. Collins, financial adviser, for her encouragement and resourceful fact-gathering; and to John Collins and Betty Hart of the Investment Company Institute, who supplied current mutual fund statistics and industry information.

As always, profound thanks to my agent, Mike Larsen, who helped focus my approach, and to my wonderful editor, Theresa Burns, for believing in me and for being the touchstone that shaped the final manuscript.

And finally, thanks to all who have attended my seminars over the years, and asked the questions that inspired this book. In many different ways, you all asked, "How can mutual funds help me?" Here, for each of you, is the answer.

. . . .

INTRODUCTION

Welcome to the exciting and profitable world of mutual funds. This book is the second in a series that began with *The Way to Save: A Ten-Step Blueprint for Lifetime Security*. *The Way to Save* tells you how to cut expenses and increase income so you can save for your goals. But how do you invest the money you have saved? That is a very important question, and *The Way to Invest* provides the answer: mutual funds.

If you are like most people, you don't want to know *all about* mutual funds: you want to know *what to do* with your money. This unique book addresses your needs in a simple, uncomplicated way. Although over one hundred books have been published about mutual funds, they are all "information-driven" rather than "investor-driven"; they focus primarily on the types of mutual funds and how they work. This book is different: it concentrates on your goals, your timetable, and your risk profile to show you how to use mutual funds to reach your financial targets. Its simple, step-by-step style focuses on the "how-to" rather than the "all about" of mutual fund investing.

The concept of mutual funds is fairly simple. A mutual fund is a pool of money from investors with goals similar to yours; this money is invested by the mutual fund manager or investment committee. You buy shares in the mutual fund, and then sit back and leave the rest to the experts, who invest your money in stocks or bonds of many different companies or government entities.

The value of your mutual fund shares depends on the value of the stocks or bonds the fund owns. When those underlying investments increase in value, the value of your shares goes up. If they go down in value, your share value will decline.

All mutual funds will pay you periodic dividends. Income dividends are your share of dividends and interest the fund receives from its holdings of stocks and bonds, minus the fund's operating expenses. Capital gain dividends are your share of profits from sales of the underlying securities. The fund will either send you a check for these dividends, or reinvest them to increase your investment in the fund. It's your choice.

Mutual Fund Investing Is Easier (and Cheaper) Than You Think

You don't have to know a great deal about investments to make money in mutual funds. All you need is a reasonable knowledge of your own financial situation and goals, and some basic guidelines for picking the right funds and avoiding major mistakes. This book is a practical guide to mutual fund investing for people who are tired of making bad investment choices, or even no choices at all.

You don't have to be rich to invest in mutual funds. As a matter of fact, most mutual fund shareholders are not rich. The median household income is $50,000, which means one-half of shareholders have income below that amount. Some mutual funds will allow you to invest $50 a month or less, so you can build a substantial portfolio over time at a reasonable cost.

Many people find investing in mutual funds confusing. Mutual funds *should* make investing easy, because the fund manager takes care of all the details of selecting, buying, and selling the stocks and bonds in which the fund invests. Unfortunately, choosing the right mutual funds is bewildering for most people. It doesn't have to be, and this book will provide you with a simple, concise guide through the mutual fund maze.

In the first part of this book you will evaluate your risk tolerance to see if you are a Defensive, an Easygoing, or a Daredevil investor. Then you will evaluate your goals to determine which investment timetable is best for you: Conserver, Builder, or Striver. Once you've identified your risk profile and timetable, you can choose the right investment mix for you from the nine investment profiles. Next you'll use the worksheets to evaluate appropriate funds and pick the funds that fit your needs. In this book you will find many unique worksheets to guide you as you choose the right mutual funds for you, and monitor their performance.

In the second part of the book, you'll learn how economic conditions affect your investments, and how to take advantage of economic cycles as you invest. You'll find out how retirement plans and tax advantages can swell the value of your investments, and where to get professional advice. Finally, you'll learn how to adjust your investments over time to meet your changing goals.

What You Won't Find in This Book

This book provides a useful overview of mutual funds and a simple process you can follow to make mutual fund investing uncomplicated. You can fashion your investment portfolio quickly and devote little time to tending it. If you are looking for a compilation of complex and erudite theories about modern portfolio management and volatility measurement, you won't find it here. There are many sophisticated financial publications available to feed your thirst for advanced knowledge about investment theories and high finance.

This book won't give you a listing of the one hundred best funds on the market today. Actually, there are far more than one hundred excellent choices, and this book will teach you how to evaluate them yourself and choose funds that suit your particular needs. You'll learn to evaluate your goals, timetable, and risk tolerance and then put your knowledge to work to enhance your financial picture.

Don't expect this book to focus solely on commission-free no-load funds and summarily dismiss load funds, which are sold by stockbrokers and other investment professionals and include a commission in their price. Stockbrokers and other financial advisers provide valuable advice and continuing support, and the funds they sell are worthy of your consideration. Load funds comprise about 50 percent of the funds from which you can choose, so it is not prudent to eliminate them from consideration. After all, you can earn far more in a high-performance load fund than in a lackluster no-load.

The Five Steps to Successful Mutual Fund Investing

This book is a five-step blueprint for investing in mutual funds. To become a successful mutual fund investor, simply follow these five steps, using the worksheets in each chapter as your guide. The five steps are:

Step 1. Understand your risk profile and identify your financial goals and investment time horizon. It is important to know whether you are a Defensive, Easygoing, or Daredevil investor by nature, and whether your timetable means you should invest as a Conserver, a Builder, or a Striver.

Step 2. Select the right asset allocation based on your risk profile, financial goals, and time horizon.

Step 3. Research funds that fit that mix, select the right funds for you, and invest.

Step 4. Keep track of your mutual funds, and add to them regularly.

Step 5. Assess your funds' performance, and modify your investments periodically.

Whether you are an investor just starting out, or an experienced investor who wants to know more about tailoring mutual funds to your own risk profile and investment timetable, this five-step blueprint should provide the important next step on your path toward financial security.

PART I

. . . .

YOUR FIVE-STEP BLUEPRINT FOR MUTUAL FUND INVESTING

1

· · · · · · · ·

MAKING MORE MONEY
WITH LESS RISK
WITH MUTUAL FUNDS

Don't put all your eggs in the same basket" is sage advice, but when applied to investments, that advice leaves many unanswered questions. For example: Which baskets should I use? How many baskets will I need? Should I put the baskets in different locations? How many eggs should I put in each basket? When I need an egg, from which basket should I take it? Should I rearrange the eggs periodically, turning them over and moving them from basket to basket? Where will I find the time to watch them all? That is why more people think about investing than actually take the plunge. "It's too complicated," they say. "I won't know what stocks to buy. I won't know when to sell. And I don't want to take huge risks with my money." So they put their nest eggs in the bank in uncomplicated certificates of deposit and savings accounts, accepting low interest rates because they are overwhelmed by the choices.

Mutual funds are a perfect way to increase the baskets for your nest eggs, reduce the risk of loss, and still keep your investments simple. There are many advantages to investing in mutual funds. Diversification among a large number of companies is the major advantage, but the ease of investing is a close second. You don't have to keep track of the underlying investments and decide when to sell one security and buy another: the fund manager will take care of that. And most funds give the fund manager the latitude to sell securities and move a portion of the portfolio into cash when the economic outlook is shaky or stocks appear to be overpriced. With the fund manager making those major decisions, all you have to do is invest your money and have patience.

Investing in mutual funds isn't time-consuming or difficult. That's because you'll have a knowledgeable team of experts on your side, to make daily decisions about whether to buy or sell. Through your mutual funds you will employ investment wizards who spend their days analyzing stocks, bonds, and market shifts, economists who filter every nuance of economic data through complex formulas, and statisticians and analysts who pore over mountains of details to track market trends and evaluate fundamental company data.

TIME AND MONEY

A recent survey revealed that for people who make over $25,000 a year, money isn't their biggest worry—time is. Though most of those surveyed were dissatisfied with their financial picture, they were even more concerned with a lack of time to get things done. Mutual funds are a smart way to save time while investing.

Types of Mutual Funds

Mutual funds come in all shapes and sizes. Although many people think of the stock market when they think of mutual funds, at the end of 1993 there were $761 billion invested in bond mutual funds and $565 billion in money market mutual funds, compared to $749 billion held in stock funds.

There are six major categories of funds:

1. Money Market Funds

These funds invest in very short-term cash and debt instruments. Many money market funds are similar to interest-bearing checking and savings accounts, allowing you to write checks against the funds you have on deposit, but the interest they pay is generally much higher than interest paid by the bank.

2. Bond Funds

Bond funds invest in bonds issued by companies, municipalities, or the U.S. government, including GNMA funds. Although bond funds are generally considered to be less risky than funds that invest in stock, the steep 1994 decline in bond prices, and the corresponding decline in value of bond mutual funds, knocked the complacency out of staid bond fund investors. Similarly, funds that invest in bonds of lesser quality, the so-called "junk" or "high-yield" bonds, have experienced frequent sharp changes in value.

Some bond funds invest your money in convertible bonds. A convertible bond, like a convertible car, serves well in many economic climates. Convertible bonds are part bond and part stock. Like any bond, they pay interest initially, but they can later be swapped for a fixed number of shares of stock. If the company's stock goes down, the convertible bond should maintain much of its value, because the interest will continue to be paid and thus will act as a cushion. If the stock goes up, the convertible bond becomes more valuable. Convertible bonds aren't as sexy as topless cars. They are generally considered to be a conservative investment vehicle, allowing you to invest in the stock market while still enjoying an initial higher yield, and thus less risk. That gives you the best of both worlds: income now, with the ability to acquire shares at a bargain price if the stock price goes up.

3. Equity Income, Growth and Income, and Index Funds

These funds invest primarily in stocks that pay dividends. For that reason, these funds tend to fluctuate less in value than growth funds, because the regular payment of quarterly dividends acts as a stabilizer for the stocks.

Because it is difficult to outperform the stock market, particularly with relatively stable large-company stocks, index funds take the easy way out and go with the flow. Index funds simply invest in the stocks included in a major index, such as the S&P 500 (which is a compilation of the average stock price of the five hundred largest publicly held corporations in America), in a mix that matches the index as closely as possible. It's all done by formula, so index funds don't need to hire an expensive fund manager to pick stocks. By keeping expenses down, they can increase returns. Indexing works less well with the more volatile small company and international stocks, where a good fund manager can often pick stocks that create stellar fund performance.

4. Growth and Maximum Growth Funds

Growth funds generally invest in stocks of large, often well-known companies that have a history of steady growth. Maximum growth funds invest in stocks of medium-size or small companies positioned to grow. Some examples of today's growth stocks include Microsoft, Intel, Wal-Mart, and Home Depot. Though the earnings of these growth stocks are expected to soar, growth stocks pay little in dividends, as their earnings are used to finance expanding operations rather than to make sizable cash distributions to shareholders. A well-known growth mutual fund is Fidelity Magellan.

Maximum growth funds invest in stocks of companies that are smaller and less well known—companies whose profits are often not currently high, but whose earnings are growing rapidly. The largest maximum growth fund is Twentieth Century Ultra.

Growth and maximum growth stocks provide some shelter from taxes, because you pay taxes only on the profits when a stock held by the portfolio is sold. If the portfolio manager holds on to the investment for many years, the growth is not taxable to you during the holding period, only upon its sale.

5. Total Return, Balanced, and Asset Allocation Funds

These invest in both stocks and bonds to blend income and growth. The percentage of fund assets invested in each category may be fixed by the fund (for example, 60 percent in stocks and 40 percent in bonds); have a specified range (for example, 35 to 65 percent in stocks and 35 to 65 percent in bonds); or be specified as a minimum or maximum (for example, at least 25 percent in bonds, or no more than 75 percent in stocks). Some total return and balanced funds, and almost all asset allocation funds, leave the asset mix percentage up to the fund manager, who shifts among categories depending on economic outlooks.

6. Specialized Funds

These invest in a single segment of the economy—such as precious metals, natural resources, technology, or real estate—or in foreign securities. Funds that invest strictly in foreign securities generally have the word *international* as part of their name, or bear the name of the country or region in which they invest: thus, for example, Oakmark International or Fidelity Latin America.

Real estate mutual funds are proliferating, as more investors want to invest in real estate without direct ownership and management responsibilities. Most of the real estate mutual funds invest in a variety of real estate investment trusts (REITs), which are companies that invest in property or mortgages. About 25 percent of REITs invest directly in properties, and thus yield partially tax-deferred dividends. The rest invest in mortgages, whose returns are not tax-deferred.

If you own your own home, don't put too much of your investment nest egg into real estate funds. As a home owner, you already have a substantial real estate investment, and the key to good investment management is diversification.

Closed-End Funds and Unit Investment Trusts

Most mutual funds are open-end, which means they accept new money from investors for new mutual fund shares, and redeem shares at the investor's request. Closed-end funds are mutual funds, just like open-end funds, but the similarity ends there. Open-end mutual funds can issue unlimited shares, but closed-end funds issue a fixed number of shares. These shares are traded like stocks on one of the major stock exchanges or on the over-the-counter market, and you buy and sell them through a commissioned broker. They generally trade at a premium or a discount, unlike open-end mutual funds, which trade at the net asset value of the underlying securities, plus a load, if applicable.

A unit investment trust (UIT) is also a mutual fund of sorts, but its investments are fixed at the beginning and don't change over the life of the trust. Unit investment trusts generally invest in bonds, although a few invest in stocks. If you invest in a unit investment trust, you know when you can expect to receive your principal, and have a good idea of how much income you will receive each month. If a bond in the portfolio is redeemed early, you will receive a portion of your principal, and your investment income from the trust will fall. UITs can be purchased through a stockbroker or directly from the trust sponsor. There is generally an up-front sales charge when you purchase a UIT, so UITs are better suited to investors who will hold the fund for ten years or longer.

The Mutual Fund Triangle

Every investment provides stability, income, or growth, but no investment provides all three. As a matter of fact, the more of one of these factors a particular fund provides, the less it will provide of the other two. Here's a mutual fund triangle that illustrates this principle.

Look at the broad base of the mutual fund triangle, with the cornerstones of "Income" and "Stability." Money market funds and bond funds lie across that base. The income you can earn from money market funds and bond funds depends on the type of investments the fund makes. For example, U.S. government money market funds are safer than regular money market funds, because the underlying investments are guaranteed by the U.S. government. Money market funds have no direct government guarantees, as do bank accounts. Even so, U.S. government money market funds are probably safer than bank accounts, because their investments are guaranteed by the full faith and credit of the U.S. government rather than by an agency of the government. Bond

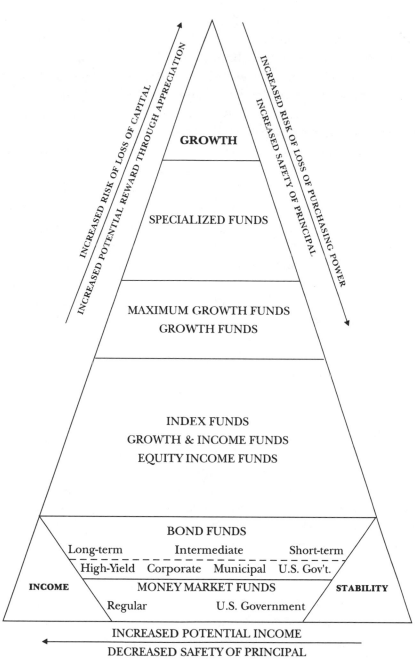

INCREASED RISK OF LOSS OF CAPITAL
INCREASED POTENTIAL REWARD THROUGH APPRECIATION

INCREASED RISK OF LOSS OF PURCHASING POWER
INCREASED SAFETY OF PRINCIPAL

GROWTH

SPECIALIZED FUNDS

MAXIMUM GROWTH FUNDS
GROWTH FUNDS

INDEX FUNDS
GROWTH & INCOME FUNDS
EQUITY INCOME FUNDS

BOND FUNDS

Long-term   Intermediate   Short-term

High-Yield   Corporate   Municipal   U.S. Gov't.

INCOME   MONEY MARKET FUNDS   **STABILITY**

Regular   U.S. Government

INCREASED POTENTIAL INCOME
DECREASED SAFETY OF PRINCIPAL

The Mutual Fund Triangle

yield (income) is similarly dependent on the type of bond, with U.S. government bonds offering the most safety and stability of principal, while high-yield bonds, also known as "junk bonds," offer less stability but greater yields. Another factor in bond yields is the term of the bond. Short-term bonds, invested for less than three years, generally pay less interest but are more stable than long-term bonds invested for ten years or more.

Now look at the top of the mutual fund triangle, at the pinnacle called "Growth." The higher you go on the triangle, the more appreciation is possible, but the farther you are from income and stability. Just as in the game of baseball, you can't steal second base and keep one foot on first; in order to shoot for maximum growth, you will have to leave the confines of the triangle's base.

If your investment objective is income and stability, you will probably invest more heavily in money market funds and short-term bond funds than in the other funds. If you are looking for long-term growth, equity (stock) funds will be your ticket. Specialized funds are more speculative, because they limit their investments to one particular segment of the economy. They can sometimes provide spectacular gains, but they can hand you crushing losses as well.

The Risks of Investing

An ideal investment would provide a high return, tax-free, with guaranteed principal, and could be cashed for full value at any time. Don't spend your time looking for this perfect "riskless investment"—it doesn't exist. There is no way you can avoid risk—it is inherent in any investment. You must decide which risks you are willing to take, and which you are best off avoiding. Fortunately, risks and rewards go hand in hand, so the more risk you are willing to take, the greater your potential reward. Unfortunately, to earn high returns you must tolerate above-average volatility, which is what most people think of when they think of risk.

Here is a chart that shows how the various types of mutual funds balance the degree of risk (volatility) with probability of return.

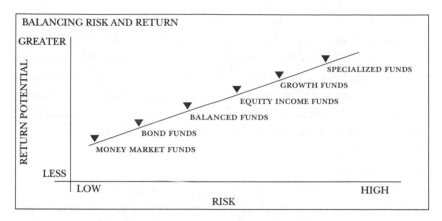

BALANCING RISK AND RETURN

As you can see, the least risky funds are the money market funds, but they also offer the lowest potential for return. As you increase return potential, you also increase risk. Growth funds have a great potential for return, but the volatility risk is greater as well.

One risk you don't have to be concerned with is the risk that your mutual fund will go broke. Because a mutual fund is a basket of securities, for it to go broke, each security it holds would have to become worthless. That is not a likely scenario. But the value of your mutual fund will fluctuate every day, depending on the closing price of the stocks or bonds that the fund holds.

For example, if the mutual fund holds 10,000 shares each of twenty different stocks, and the closing price is up $1 per share for half the stocks and down $1 per share for the other half, your mutual fund value per share will stay the same. But if the price increases were greater than the declines, then your fund value per share will increase. If the underlying stocks lost more value than they gained that day, the price of your fund shares will decline.

Inflation Risk
In a book called *Run Toward the Roar,* an African missionary told of seeing gazelles grazing in a field. As she watched, a pride of lions silently surrounded the field. When all of the lions were in place, as if by signal, two old, toothless lions roared very loudly. The frightened gazelles swiftly stampeded away from the roar—and straight into the mouths of the younger waiting lions.

It is natural to fear risk—fear is part of our instinct for survival; but take a lesson from the gazelles and focus on the *real* risks that affect you. Calculate how much your savings earn, then subtract inflation and taxes, and you will find you are losing money each year by investing in certificates of deposit, savings accounts, and money funds. Certainly, there is a chance you will lose money in a particular year if you invest in equity mutual funds, but keeping money "safe in the bank" is even riskier, as it guarantees you will lose money *every* year.

Because you want your money to last as long as you do, you are probably a long-term investor who will keep much of your money invested for ten years or longer. As a long-term investor, you can afford to take a considerable amount of risk with your money before it equals the inflation risk you inevitably face. Unfortunately, it is human nature to consider what you know to be safe and what you don't know to be risky, and you are probably far more familiar with savings accounts and certificates of deposit than with mutual funds. But if you flee from the toothless threat of volatility, you will run straight into the jaws of inflation.

Even if inflation continues at only 3 to 4 percent each year, over the next twenty years your money will lose more than 50 percent of its value, because at that rate of inflation, things will cost twice as much in twenty years as they do now. And you can bet that inflation will continue; it's nothing new. Franklin P. Adams, a social commentator in the early part of the twentieth century, once remarked, "There are plenty of good five-cent cigars in the country, but the trouble is they cost a quarter. What this country really needs is a good five-cent *nickel*." He'd be shocked at how little a nickel is worth today, and prices will continue to climb.

Stocks are considered by many people to be risky investments, but they are tame when compared to the risks of inflation. Stocks, in this century, have never lost even 1 percent of their value over a twenty-year period, never mind losing 50 percent. Most investors are too cautious with their money. Inflation risk is the biggest financial hazard the long-term investor faces.

A long-term time horizon overcomes the risk of volatility. Although your mutual fund returns may fluctuate widely year by year, the average return over a long term is pretty predictable. For example, since 1929, the best year for stock market gains was 1933, when stocks gained 54 percent. But just two years earlier, in 1931, stocks lost 43 percent, the worst year in modern history. An overly cautious investor, spooked by the stock market crash in 1929 and the steep decline of 1931, would have been sitting on the sidelines and missed the greatest stock market gains in history. The more years you have to invest, the better the odds that your total stock market return will approximate the long-term average return of stocks, a satisfying 10.3 percent.

HOW INFLATION AFFECTS YOU

At just 4 percent inflation, here is what $1,000 will buy in the future, in today's dollars.

Years Elapsed	Buying Power of $1,000
0	$1,000
5	822
10	676
15	555
20	456
25	375
30	308
35	253
40	208
45	171
50	141

The short-term investor, who will need his money in three years or less, will generally be better off accepting inflation risk in favor of increased stability, because over the short term inflation won't affect purchasing power much. But the long-term investor would be better off accepting the investment risks of the stock market to overcome inflation risk, because the long-term investor has enough time to enjoy the ups and weather the downs. Before you sign on for the ride, however, make sure you are indeed committed for the long haul. If you buy mutual funds that invest in stocks and bonds, you may be sure that your portfolio will fluctuate in value, sometimes dropping dramatically. If you panic and sell when prices are down, you will have converted your investments from long-term to short-term. If there is a chance you will have to liquidate your holdings in the near future, then you must follow strategies for short-term investors rather than for mid-term or long-term investors.

Income Risk

For the investor, a major risk is the possibility that you will make less return than you expected. That risk appears in every investment. If you invested in certificates of deposit during the early 1980s, when interest rates were in the high teens, you might have expected those rates would continue forever. What a disappointment the 2 to 3 percent interest rates of the early 1990s were in light of those expectations! If you invested in lesser-quality junk bonds in the mid-1980s, hoping that taking more risk would increase your returns, you might have been disappointed when you lost part of your principal, which dashed your hopes for a great return. You had merely substituted one form of risk for another.

Volatility Risk

Although stocks and bonds are called "securities," it would be a mistake to think of them as "secure." Both stocks and bonds are prone to price swings or income fluctuations, which are called *volatility risks*. Stocks and bonds share two volatility risks: *company risk*, which is the risk that an individual company will suffer serious financial misfortunes, and *market risk*, which is the risk that the market will go down (a bear market) rather than up (a bull market).

Research shows that by holding from twelve to twenty different stocks in a portfolio, most company risk can be eliminated; by investing in mutual funds, you will eliminate most serious company risk. Market risk, on the other hand, is "nondiversifiable," so in a bear market mutual funds will go down just like everything else. Fortunately, time is on your side: bear markets always end. (Unfortunately, so do bull markets, but they generally last much longer than bear markets.) The only thing that truly reduces market risk is time: being a long-term investor has advantages in overcoming market risk.

The best way to handle volatility risk is to set reasonable expectations, allocate strategically among the different types of investments available, and then give your investments time to grow. The more time involved, the more closely the average return on investments will approximate the expected return.

If, on the other hand, you are saving for a short-term goal, such as a down payment on a home in a couple of years, or a cruise vacation next year, inflation isn't much of a risk. Volatility in the stock market is a far greater risk for the short-term investor than is inflation, so the short-term investor should keep money safely in the bank or invested in money market funds.

THE BULLS AND THE BEARS

When Wall Street talks about the bulls and the bears, what do those terms mean? Bulls thrust upward with their horns: a bull market is one that is aggressively moving upward. Bears, on the other hand, claw downward when they attack. A bear market is in decline, moving generally in a downward direction.

HOW VOLATILITY RISK IS MEASURED

When most people think of risk, they think of volatility. The greater the price swings or income fluctuations from an investment, the greater the risk that the value of their investment will jump around and that the returns will be erratic. These risks are calculated by sophisticated measures called *standard deviation* and *beta*.

Standard deviation measures how much the return on an investment will deviate from its expected return over the years, as market conditions change. The higher the number, the greater the volatility of returns. An investment that never varied would have a standard deviation of 1. Most stock funds have a standard deviation of 9 or above, so their returns can be extremely volatile. Bond funds are generally in the 2 to 8 range, depending on the type of bond, investment grade, and maturity. For example, a short-term U.S. Treasury bond fund would have a low standard deviation, while a junk bond fund invested in lower-rated securities would have a high standard deviation.

Beta measures how much the price of the mutual fund fluctuates relative to the Standard & Poor's 500 stock index, with 1 representing the market. A fund that has a beta of .7 fluctuates less than the overall market, while a fund with a beta of 2 fluctuates twice as much as the market, giving you a colossal roller coaster ride (with thrills most investors would rather avoid). Equity income funds would have a low beta, while many maximum growth funds have high betas.

You won't encounter these terms very often, so there is no need to memorize these definitions. Mutual fund listings in magazines and newspapers often rank funds not only by total return, but also by risk. Standard deviation and beta are the two measures of risk that are most frequently used to calculate those risks.

ANNUALIZED RETURNS

Here are the fifteen-year annualized returns for funds (as of June 30, 1994), and the volatility score (with 10 being the volatility of the S&P 500 stock index:

	Return	Volatility
Aggressive growth stock funds	13.6	13.7
Long-term growth stocks	14.2	11.2
Growth and income stocks	13.0	8.2
High-yield corporate bonds	10.9	5.4
Corporate bond funds	9.9	4.1
Government bond funds	9.0	4.0

Opportunity Risk and Reinvestment Risk

Another risk is *opportunity risk*, which is the risk that your money will be tied up elsewhere when a better investment opportunity comes along, or that you will miss an upswing in the market. The flip side is *reinvestment risk*, which is the risk that at the time investment income is paid to you or your money is returned to you, you won't be able to invest it at a rate of earnings as good as before. This risk became very real to those who invested in 1980 in certificates of deposit or bonds paying 18 percent or more, which were later redeemed when interest rates had dipped below 10 percent.

Credit Risk

Credit risk is a special risk that bond investors face. It is the chance that your investments will be affected by a change in the credit-worthiness of the institution that backs your investments, such as a downgrade in the credit quality of California municipal bonds, or the bankruptcy of Penn Central.

Other Investment Risks

As if all these risks weren't enough, there are some other investment risks of which you should be aware. These risks include rising interest rates, poor financial performance of a company, and defaults by bond issuers. Fortunately, these risks can be tempered if you take certain precautions.

• **Rising interest rates** can be combatted by investing in bond funds with short-term (up to three years) or intermediate-term (three to ten years) maturity dates. That way, as interest rates rise, your funds will have bonds maturing at regular intervals, and the redemption proceeds can be invested in bonds with the new higher interest rates. A word of caution, though: If you expect interest rates to decline, you'll want to invest in long-term bond funds with bond maturities of ten years or longer, to lock in the current higher interest rates.

• **Poor financial performance** of a company can be mitigated through diversification among several different companies in a variety of industries. Most mutual funds hold dozens of different stocks in many sectors of the economy, so mutual funds are a natural vehicle for overcoming this risk.

• **Possible bond defaults** can be generally avoided by investing in funds that hold U.S. government bonds or AAA-rated corporate bonds. Another way of protecting against bond defaults is to invest in funds that hold insured bonds (which are insured against default in principal or interest payments), or prefunded bonds, which are guaranteed by a pool of funds that has been set aside for their eventual redemption. But be aware that by girding yourself against risk, you are also giving up income. Insured and prefunded bonds yield less than do other bonds; corporate bonds with lower ratings pay higher interest, and in a strong economy offer the potential for value increases as well.

HOW TO CONTROL RISK

Here is a list of the various types of investment risks and what you can do to control them.

Type of Risk	How to Control Risk
Inflation Risk	Invest for greater potential return
Income Risk	Diversify bond maturities
Company Risk	Invest in 20 different stocks, or a mutual fund
Market Risk	Invest for the long term
Opportunity Risk	Allocate assets properly
Reinvestment Risk	Diversify bond maturities
Credit Risk	Diversify bond issuers
Rising Interest Rates	Invest in short- or intermediate-term bonds
Falling Interest Rates	Invest in long-term bonds
Poor Financial Performance	Diversify among different industries
Possible Bond Defaults	Invest in high-grade or insured bond funds

---

Most risk can be summarized in two basic questions:

1. Will I get my money back?
2. Will my investments outpace inflation?

It is natural to want to avoid risk; it is also natural to believe that any investment with which you are familiar and comfortable is safe, and all others are risky. Be sure that your intolerance for risk isn't influenced by a lack of investment knowledge. Once you are aware that every investment has risk, even the ones with which you have before felt safe, you may be more willing to venture into unknown areas that offer you better financial protection. As you determine your risk tolerance, consider your stage in life, your financial goals, your income level, your tax situation, your personal financial outlook, and the outlook of the economy in general. In future chapters you will learn how to evaluate these elements and integrate them into a mutual fund investment plan for you.

Through the diversification possible with mutual funds, and by maintaining a long-term horizon, you can take greater risks for greater reward. Time and diversification will mitigate the risks while compounding the rewards.

2

· · · · · · · ·

STEP I
Identify Your Risk Profile,
Goals, and Time Horizon

Many people turn to magazines or other financial guides to tell them how they should invest their money. Unfortunately, those guides are generic, with advice generally based on your age. "If you are in your thirties," they say, "here's how you should invest." But one couple in their thirties might be expecting their first child, while another couple the same age may already be paying college bills for their firstborn. One investor may be part of a high-income two-earner couple, while another might be a single parent struggling to make it on her own.

The one-size-fits-all philosophy just doesn't make sense when it comes to finances. Investing should be based on who you are— your goals, your personal financial outlook, your family's need for support, and your own tax picture.

Before you begin planning your investment strategy, review your overall finances. Do you need current investment income? Can you add to your investments on a regular basis? How much do you need for an emergency fund? Are you investing for long-term goals, such as for retirement? Are taxes a concern for you?

Your Risk Profile

What kind of investor are you: Defensive, Easygoing, or Daredevil? It is important to know, so you can make mutual fund investments that let you feel secure. You want to be able both to sleep well *and* eat well. In Chapter 3 you will find nine possible investment allocations for your mutual fund portfolio. Which one you choose will depend in part on your risk profile. Here are two simple exercises to determine which of the three risk profiles applies to you.

STAY-ing Power

To determine your risk profile, first focus on "STAY-ing power." Investments have four basic attributes whose first letters combine to spell *STAY*: stability, tax savings, appreciation (growth), and yield (income). All investments have one or more of these attributes, but no investment has all four. How much of each attribute you need depends on your current financial picture and your own personal goals.

For example, take two investors in their early forties. One, a widow, is a teacher with two teenagers still at home. The other investor is married, and also has two teenagers, but he is a cardiologist in private practice, at the peak of his earning years. The widow will likely need more stability and income, while the surgeon will be looking for growth and tax savings. These two investors are the same age, and each has children who will go to college soon. The similarities end there. College expenses will be easily affordable for the surgeon, but will strain the widow's budget. Their needs for the various investment attributes are very different, influenced not just by their ages and family size, but also by their needs for liquidity, their earnings, their abilities to take risks, and their tax situations.

What combination of STAY-ing power is right for you? To decide, assign a total of ten points among the four factors, giving the most points to the factors that are most important to you, but assigning no more than four points to any single factor.

If stability is paramount for you, you'll assign that factor four points, and therefore have to assign the other factors fewer points. If you need current income, yield may garner four points, so you'll shave points from the other goals. If you are investing for retirement, appreciation is most important, with tax benefits a close second.

If you assigned more points to stability and yield, and fewer to tax savings and appreciation, you are probably a Defensive investor. If most of your points were assigned to yield and appreciation, you are probably an Easygoing investor. If your points leaned heavily toward appreciation and tax savings, you are a Daredevil investor.

Stability	_____
Tax savings	_____
Appreciation	_____
Yield	_____
Total	10

The Risk Quiz

Now take this quiz to further explore your risk profile.

Each item in the following pairs represents the extreme end of the spectrum. Assign a number between 1 and 5, as follows:

1. I agree with statement A.
2. I mostly agree with statement A.
3. I agree/disagree equally with statements A and B.
4. I mostly agree with statement B.
5. I agree with statement B.

QUESTION 1:

A. I would rather earn less on my money in exchange for greater stability and less risk.

B. I don't mind the annual return of my investments fluctuating greatly over the years, as long as I make above-average returns overall.

QUESTION 2:

A. I would like to make an average of 12 percent a year on my money, but it would distress me terribly if I lost 12 percent in any particular year.

B. My primary goal is maximum long-term capital growth, and I don't care how many risks I must take to get it.

QUESTION 3:

A. I am investing money I have been given, won in a lawsuit, etc., and I would never be able to replace it if I lost it.

B. If I lose money, I have plenty of income to replace it.

QUESTION 4:

A. I am nervous about investing in the stock market, because I feel it is very risky.

B. I am afraid of high inflation, and I want to protect the future buying power of my money.

QUESTION 5:

A. If I invested my money for five years, I would be satisfied if it just kept up with inflation.

B. If I invested my money for five years, I would expect it to at least double in value.

QUESTION 6:

A. I like to keep a lot of money accessible in my checking and savings accounts because I never know when I might need it.

B. I earn enough money to take care of my daily needs, and I'd like to have my money invested for maximum growth.

Now add up your points. If you scored 6 to 12, you are a Defensive investor. If you scored 13 to 23, you are an Easygoing investor. And if you scored 24 to 30, you are a Daredevil investor.

The Risk Quiz measured your attitude toward risk, while the STAY-ing power exercise measured your perceived ability to take risks. You may find that your score in the Risk Quiz characterized you as a different type of investor than your answers to the STAY-ing power exercise. For example, the surgeon in the STAY-ing power example perceived his needs to be for growth and tax savings, making him a Daredevil investor. And yet he may be afraid of risk, and so his total score on the Risk Quiz was only 11, meaning he is a Defensive investor.

Or consider the widow in the same example. Although she needs stability and income from her investments, making her a Defensive investor, perhaps she is a natural-born risk-taker. Her score of 26 on the Risk Quiz showed her to be a Daredevil.

If your scores are skewed, what should you do? First, reread the section on general risks in Chapter 1, to be sure you understand that all investments have risk. Then review the Risk Quiz again to see if you would change any of your answers.

Now review your answers in the STAY-ing power exercise. Think carefully about your age, your liquidity needs, your earning power, and your tax situation. Does your apportionment of points reflect your true situation?

Once you have reviewed and adjusted your answers, see if your risk profiles are still out of kilter. If so, pay some attention to your Risk Quiz profile, but give more weight to the STAY-ing power exercise, as that reflects your ability to take risks in your current financial situation. For example, the surgeon has the financial ability to take risks, which should make him a Daredevil investor, but he is conservative by nature, which steers him toward a Defensive posture. For now, he might compromise on the profile for Easygoing investors. The widow with Daredevil tendencies may decide to invest most of her money defensively, and follow her Daredevil bent with the rest.

The Importance of Your Time Horizon

Your time horizon is the most important element in determining the appropriate asset allocation for you. Your time horizon determines whether you should choose the portfolio mixes you will find in Chapter 3 for a Conserver, a Builder, or a Striver.

If your goal is fewer than three years away, you are a Conserver, and you must settle for a lower rate of return that provides more stability (less risk of losing money). On the other hand, if your goal is more than ten years away, you can withstand substantial market ups and downs. You are a Striver, and you will want to lean heavily toward stocks, which are more volatile but provide substantially better odds of high returns than other types of investments.

If your goal is somewhere between three and ten years away, you are a Builder. You don't want your money to languish in low-interest money market funds, and yet you don't have the time to withstand the ups and downs of a volatile investment.

For example, the money you need for next year's vacation or to pay income taxes next April 15 should nestle safely in a money market fund. It won't earn much in interest, but you won't have to worry about your investment losing value; it will be there when you need it. But a money market fund would be a foolish place to put the money you intend for retirement in fifteen years. Retirement money should be invested for long-term growth. Although growth funds fluctuate widely from month to month and year to year, over time the upward fluctuations cancel out the downward ticks. You have a great opportunity to make your money grow in a growth fund, but not much potential for return in a money market fund, which will generally only keep up with inflation.

Approach your investments from the vantage point of an eagle, not an ant. The eagle can see the road ribbon smoothly into the future. An ant can see only the imperfections in the surface, and each peak and valley looks almost insurmountable. So it is with market fluctuations: each week your mutual funds will vacillate up and down, giving antlike investors the anxious jitters; but over several years, an eagle's perspective will show a ribbon of steady growth.

Don't underestimate your time horizon, or you will subject yourself to enormous risks. Short-term bond funds or money market funds, which are considered "conservative" investments, are highly appropriate for short time horizons. But these same investments pose major risks to long-term investors, in the form of inflation.

Money market funds provide stability of principal at the inevitable risk that your money will lose buying power. That is no problem over the short term, but would be a major problem long-term. On the other hand, stock market volatility is a short-term risk, which diminishes to zero over a number of years. That is why equity (stock) funds are the most appropriate investment for those with long time horizons.

If you are planning for retirement, don't confuse your retirement horizon with your time horizon. Your time horizon is not limited to just the years until retirement: your investments must last many years into retirement as well. A more appropriate gauge of your time horizon is your remaining life expectancy, rather than the number of years until you retire.

Putting It All Together

Now that you have identified your risk profile, explored your goals, and pegged your time horizon, it is time to put it all together. Your risk profile and financial situation identify you as a Defensive, Easygoing, or Daredevil investor. Your time horizon dictates whether you are a Conserver, a Builder, or a Striver. Putting it together, you can now classify yourself. If you are saving for a child's education in ten years (Builder), and your risk profile is of a moderate bent (Easygoing), you are an Easygoing Builder. If you are saving for the long-term goal of retirement (Striver), but you are definitely not a risk-taker (Defensive), then you are a Defensive

Striver. A risk-taker by nature (Daredevil) who is saving for a short-term goal, such as a new house in a couple of years (Conserver), is a Daredevil Conserver.

Using these profiles as a guide, there are nine possible combinations that will describe you and your financial goals. Here is a matrix of the possibilities:

Defensive Conserver	Defensive Builder	Defensive Striver
Easygoing Conserver	Easygoing Builder	Easygoing Striver
Daredevil Conserver	Daredevil Builder	Daredevil Striver

In the next chapter you will find out how to structure a portfolio that will fit your needs, whichever of these nine profiles fits you.

What Are Your Financial Goals?

Some common financial goals include creating a cash reserve for emergencies, saving for a special vacation, buying a new car, making a down payment on a new home, financing a new business, educating children, and retirement. Make a list of the financial goals that concern you, how many years you have to save for them, what they will cost in today's dollars, and how much you have already saved. For example, your list might look like this:

Financial Goal	Years Left	Cost	Saved
Down payment for home	4	$ 15,000	$ 5,000
Educate children	15	50,000	10,000
Retirement	30	500,000	70,000

To determine how much you will need to save each month to meet those goals, first subtract the amount you have already saved for the goal from the cost. Then divide the result by the appropriate number from the following table:

TABLE 2.1
YOUR RISK PROFILE

Years to goal	Defensive	Easygoing	Daredevil
2	25	25	26
4	52	54	56
6	81	86	92
8	113	123	134
10	147	164	183
15	245	291	347
20	365	462	592
25	511	693	957
30	689	1005	1503
35	906	1425	2317
40	1170	1992	3532

If you are an Easygoing investor you will need to invest $185 per month ($10,000 divided by 54) to meet your goal for a new home. College education of the children will take $137 per month ($40,000 divided by 291), and retirement will require a $428 monthly investment ($430,000 divided by 1005).

An investor who is saving for several goals at the same time—a new house, a child's education in ten years, and retirement in thirty years—might have three different investment plans for different segments of his or her savings.

In the example above, it will require $185 per month to save for a new home in four years, $137 per month to fund the children's education in fifteen years, and $428 per month to meet your retirement goals in thirty years. That is a total of $750 per month, which may be twice as much as you are able to save right now. What should you do if you don't have enough income to save for all three goals? You might be tempted to save only for the nearest goal, the new house, and delay saving for the children's education and retirement. But that will put you way behind in a few years in funding for those goals, and you will later regret having put off investing for them. Here is a better way of integrating your goals with your limited resources.

First, take a hard look at your goals. Do you really need a new home, or can you make adequate improvements to the old one rather than moving up? Do your children really need to go to private schools, or will the state university system give them a decent education at a fraction of the cost? And is retirement at sixty-two really important for you, or could you work until you are sixty-eight, giving yourself six more years to save for retirement?

If the amount needed for your goals and their timetables can't be changed, it is time to look at your budget. Goals that are really important to you are worthy of current lifestyle sacrifices, so call a family powwow and see where each family member can scale back expenses or increase current income. Brown-bagging it to work for a few years and eating out less won't seem a major concession when you think of the joy a new house will bring. Perhaps older children can work part-time to supplement their college funds. And with a long-term goal such as retirement, you can devise a plan of steadily increasing monthly investments to help you ease into your plan. For example, if you can invest only $200 per month now toward that goal, can you increase your monthly investment to $250 next year and $300 the year after that? In a few years your retirement savings will be right on track.

Use the following worksheet to summarize your goals and investment profile.

WORKSHEET WORKSHEET 2.1

Your risk profile (Defensive, Easygoing, or Daredevil) _____

Your financial goal _____

Years left to save for goal _____

Your time horizon (Conserver, Builder, or Striver) _____

Cost of goal in today's dollars _____

Amount you can invest now _____

Amount you need to invest each month _____

Complete a worksheet for each of your investment goals.

QUESTIONS ABOUT YOUR FINANCIAL GOALS

To structure a portfolio that is allocated correctly for you, you must first define your financial goals. Ask yourself the following questions:

- What am I saving for?
- How many years do I have to save?
- How much am I targeting for an investment return?
- How prone am I to seasickness when my investments fluctuate?
- Do I need current income from my investments?
- How soon will I need the proceeds from my investments?
- How will inflation affect me?
- How much risk am I willing to take?
- How do taxes affect my investments?

Now you are ready to select the right investment mix for you, and to invest your money in funds that suit your particular needs. You may not yet feel as though you have all the answers. You never will. As James Thurber once said, "It is better to know some of the questions than all of the answers." In this chapter you have asked the right questions, found some of the answers, and you are ready to choose a variety of funds that fit your own investment profile. What the author Samuel Butler said of life is equally true of investing: it is like playing a violin in public and learning the instrument as you go along. Your confidence will grow as your experience builds.

3

· · · · · · · ·

STEP 2
Select the Right Fund Mix

Why Asset Allocation Is Important

Asset allocation is just a fancy term for divvying up your money. Unsophisticated investors often approach the process in a haphazard manner, investing a little here and a little there, with no strategy, like the man who jumped on his horse and rode madly off in all directions. That's a shame, because asset allocation—how to divide your money among the different types of funds—is the most important investment decision you'll make.

For example, if you had invested entirely in bond funds during the past thirty years, your investments would have grown 8 percent a year. But if you had invested in stocks instead, your money would have grown 11.5 percent—nearly 50 percent more.

Studies show that 92 percent of your investment return depends on the way in which you allocate your money among the different types of funds, and only 8 percent of your success depends on the actual funds in which you invest. In other words, once you decide the percentage of your money that is going to go into each type of fund, you could use a dartboard to pick the particular funds without affecting your return much. (I wouldn't recommend the dartboard approach, though. It's smart to be as careful in picking the funds as you are in allocating your assets.)

ASSET ALLOCATION PORTFOLIOS

Most investors have both short-term and long-term goals, and a mix of different mutual funds is in order. This mix is called a *portfolio,* and determining and sustaining the proper mix is called *asset allocation.*

Proper asset allocation is a good way to manage risk. It is impossible to devise a perfect asset allocation that eliminates risk and maximizes profits, but you can come reasonably close. Modern portfolio theory, the cornerstone of asset allocation, says that if you invest your money so that when one investment is down, another is likely to rise, your overall portfolio return will be steadier than if you put all your nest eggs into one type of investment basket. For example, as inflation hovers and interest rates rise, the value of your bond mutual fund will fall, but the value of your utility stock fund and real estate fund may rise correspondingly. In times of political crisis, stock fund prices might tumble, but gold funds may soar.

When people think about financial risk, they often envision their investment losing value or even disappearing altogether. For many people, the thought of this downside risk is alarming, and avoiding it becomes more important than the return they earn. That's why they put their money into low-interest savings accounts and certificates, accepting low interest rates while passing up the higher returns of more volatile investments. However, if they considered the certainty of inflation when they thought about downside risk, they would realize that inflation gnawing away at principal at a rate of 3 to 5 percent a year is far riskier to the long-term investor than the potential for a bear market. Bear markets end, but inflation will plague us forever.

Ibbotson Associates Consulting Group of Chicago predicts that over the next ten years stocks will rise 12.3 percent annually, bonds will grow 6.6 percent, and Treasury bills will yield 4.7 percent. Does that mean you should invest all your money in stocks? Probably not. For example, if you will need some of your money in just a few years, stocks may be too volatile for your entire nest egg. Although stocks may return 12.3 percent over the next ten years, in any particular year you can count on the return being either greater or less than that, and often by a wide margin. For example, in 1994, savings accounts paid only 2 percent or so interest, but that was better than the average return on stocks and bonds, which hovered a bit below zero. If you are saving for a new home in a year or two, don't put all your money into stocks. If the stock market turns bearish, you won't have time to weather the bear market to take advantage of a strong bull market. That means that when you sell your stocks to fund your down payment, you may, in the words of Shakespeare, "exit, pursued by a bear"— and find that you earned far less than you would have in a savings account. You may even have lost principal. Of course, you might also get lucky and encounter a strong bull market that produces great investment returns during the year or two your money is invested—but is that a chance you are willing to take? Most investors find the pain of losing money far sharper than the joys of above-average returns.

People often take a hodgepodge approach to their investments—even those people who read the financial magazines and reports and keep up with the latest performance of mutual funds, and thus consider themselves astute investors. They often invest in the hottest-performing mutual funds without first reviewing their goals to determine their time horizon. They may take unnecessary risks, or else play it too safe by not taking risks they *can* afford. There are plenty of solid mutual funds out there, but not every fund is right for every investor.

Some people are unrealistic about the returns that are possible from an investment mix that is appropriate for their time horizon or risk profile, and they strive for more growth from their investments than is possible. These unrealistic expectations lead people with shorter time horizons or more conservative risk profiles to choose mutual funds that have great potential for gains, without paying enough attention to the short-term risks involved.

Nine Investor Profiles

In the pages that follow, you will find suggested mutual fund allocations based on whether your goals and time horizon make you a Conserver, a Builder, or a Striver, and whether you are Defensive, Easygoing, or Daredevil in your investment approach.

Conventional wisdom says that younger people should invest more aggressively (Daredevil Strivers) and older people should be very conservative with their money (Defensive Conservers). This "wisdom" is based on the theory that young people have many years to make their money grow, and so they can withstand the ups and downs of a volatile market. Older folks, so goes the theory, have limited time and so can't cope with the roller coaster of equity investments. In reality, younger investors are often saving for short-term goals, such as the purchase of a home or the capital to start a business, and so must avoid volatility in favor of stability. Rather than being Daredevil Strivers, they should invest as Defensive Conservers. And older folks, investing for retirement, have thirty or more years ahead of them—inflation can be their worst enemy if they don't invest for growth. They should invest some of their money as Daredevil Strivers, or at the very least take the middle road of Easygoing Builders.

The Conserver (Less Than Three Years to Goal)

If you are saving for a goal for which you'll need your money within the next three years, you are a Conserver, and stability must be paramount. You must be able to cash in your investment for at least as much as you invested. As Mark Twain once said, "I am not so concerned about the return *on* my money as the return *of* my money." But Conservers would like to receive some income as well, so yield is also important. Tax benefits and appreciation are of less importance.

ULTRA-DEFENSIVE CONSERVER

If you'll need your money in a year or less, you may simply want to park it in a money market mutual fund comprised of U.S.

government obligations. Your principal will be stable; each dollar you invest will always be worth one dollar. The income your money earns will fluctuate daily as interest rates go up or down. You can add to your stash at any time, and you can withdraw it at any time.

DEFENSIVE CONSERVER

A Defensive Conserver who won't need the money quite so soon may consider adding short-term bond funds, both domestic and foreign, to the mix. If you are a Defensive Conserver, here is a mutual fund mix that would suit your goals:

Money market fund	50%
Short-term bond fund	40%
International short-term bond fund	10%

The potential income return is greater than what is obtainable by investing only in money market mutual funds, though the stability is less, because principal fluctuates up and down within a fairly narrow range.

EASYGOING CONSERVER

If you are an Easygoing Conserver, you should add some stocks to your asset mix to allow for some potential of equity growth. Here is a good asset allocation for you:

Money market fund	30%
Short-term bond fund	40%
International short-term bond fund	15%
Equity income fund	15%

DAREDEVIL CONSERVER

If you are more aggressive, a Daredevil Conserver, you may wish to put a portion of your short-term money into slightly more aggressive growth mutual funds. But remember, to obtain higher income you are risking some stability, so remain somewhat conservative or moderate with most of your money. Here is a portfolio for a Daredevil Conserver:

Money market fund	20%
Short-term bond fund	30%
International short-term bond fund	20%
Equity income fund	15%
Growth fund	15%

The Builder (Three to Ten Years to Goal)

The Builder is saving for a goal that is three to ten years away, such as college education for a child, or money to start a business. A Builder may also be someone in the later years of retirement, generally seventy-five years old or older. Or perhaps the Builder is facing a period of financial uncertainty, such as debilitating illness or possible job loss in a few years, and so may need access to invested funds.

DEFENSIVE BUILDER

The Defensive Builder will want stability, but recognizes the need for growth as well. Remember, inflation will reduce the buying power of money by about 25 percent in the next ten years. Defensive Builders should invest in a combination of funds, weighted heavily toward intermediate bond funds, but also including an international bond fund and some growth and income funds. This asset mix is good for a Defensive Builder, or a Builder who will need the invested funds in five years or less:

Intermediate bond fund	30%
International bond fund	20%
Balanced fund	25%
Growth and income fund	10%
Growth fund	10%
International equity fund	5%

EASYGOING BUILDER

The Easygoing Builder should invest less in bonds and somewhat more in equities. If your goals make you an Easygoing Builder, here is a portfolio that will suit your needs:

International bond fund	15%
Balanced fund	45%
Growth fund	15%
Maximum growth fund	10%
International equity fund	15%

DAREDEVIL BUILDER

A more aggressive Daredevil Builder will probably take greater volatility risks by investing more in equities. Daredevil Builders should take care to scale back their investments to the more protective position of Easygoing Builders as they draw closer to the date they will need their funds, and to the position of Conservers when their need for the funds is three years away or less. If you are a Daredevil Builder with more than five years until you'll need your money, here is a good portfolio for you:

International bond fund	10%
Balanced fund	30%
Growth fund	20%
Maximum growth fund	20%
International equity fund	20%

The Striver (Ten Years or More to Goal)

If you are a Striver, you can risk more volatility because time is on your side. "But I'm not a risk-taker," you may say. "I'd rather not take chances with my money." Unfortunately, inflation is the biggest risk to the Striver, and even a Defensive Striver cannot afford that risk. If you have long-term goals but invest as would a Conserver, inflation will rob your money of its buying power. For example, if you are fifty years old and expect to live another thirty-plus years, you will find that inflation will steal 60 percent of your money's buying power over your remaining years. If you are forty, 75 percent of your principal will evaporate in your lifetime. Even though the principal will remain intact, its buying power will erode. In addition, the income your investments generate will buy less and less. In twenty years everything will cost twice as much, so your money will go only half as far.

The Striver needs appreciation, appreciation, and more appreciation. Income is of less importance, because it requires giving up growth. Stability isn't as important, because over time the volatility of growth investments evens out, and the ups and downs meld into a line of steady growth.

DEFENSIVE STRIVER

The Defensive Striver probably wants more stability, and isn't willing to ride the volatility roller coaster without a seat belt. Though amenable to investing over half the portfolio in stocks, the Striver will also want to invest in domestic and international bonds. Here is a suitable portfolio for a Defensive Striver:

Intermediate bond fund	15%
International bond fund	10%
Balanced fund	25%
Growth fund	20%
Maximum growth fund	15%
International equity fund	15%

EASYGOING STRIVER

Easygoing Strivers will accept more volatility in exchange for greater potential return. Their portfolios will lean more heavily toward stocks, with less invested in domestic and international bonds. If you are an Easygoing Striver, here is the asset mix for you:

Intermediate bond fund	10%
International bond fund	10%
Balanced fund	15%
Growth fund	25%
Maximum growth fund	20%
International equity fund	20%

DAREDEVIL STRIVER

A Daredevil Striver doesn't mind the bumpy ride, and will invest most of his or her money in domestic and foreign stocks. The most aggressive Daredevil Strivers may even opt to invest 100 percent of their funds in equities. If you are not quite *that* aggressive, but a Daredevil nonetheless, here's a portfolio mix that might suit you:

Intermediate bond fund	10%
Growth fund	30%
Maximum growth fund	30%
International equity fund	30%

Where Is Your Money Now?

Once you have chosen the asset mix that is right for you, figure out how your assets are presently invested. Account for all your investments, including IRAs, 401(k) plans, TSAs, certificates of deposit and savings accounts, and brokerage accounts. Worksheet 3.1 will help you do this.

WORKSHEET 3.1
YOUR INVESTMENT ASSETS

1. CASH

Bank accounts   _____
Certificates of deposit   _____
Cash on hand   _____
Money market mutual funds   _____
                          Total cash   _____

2. INSURANCE

Cash value of whole life policies   _____
Universal life policies   _____
Variable annuities   _____
Fixed annuities   _____
                  Total insurance investments   _____

3. RETIREMENT INVESTMENTS
Individual retirement accounts (IRAs)   _____
Keogh plans   _____
SEP-IRAs   _____
Profit-sharing plans   _____
401(k) plans   _____
Tax-sheltered annuities (TSAs)   _____
                        Total retirement investments _____

4. OTHER INVESTMENTS
Stocks   _____
Bonds   _____
Mutual funds   _____
Investment real estate   _____
Investment club share   _____
Notes and mortgages receivable   _____
Other investments   _____
                        Total other investments   _____
                        Total investments   _____

Now review the asset mix of your investments on Worksheet 3.1. For each line, jot down the asset types that best describe the investment. For example, review the latest statement from your 401(k) plan, and list the types of funds (growth, bonds, money market, etc.) and the amounts invested in each. Do the same for each of your other investments, then total all the investments of each type to see what percentage of your investments is in each asset type. You can then compare your current investments with the ideal portfolio mix you identified earlier in this chapter, and begin to restructure your investments, either by selling portions of your investments and reinvesting in other asset types, or by gradually adding to your investments in underfunded asset types.

Adding More Diversification

Diversification is important, not only among different mutual fund categories, such as stock funds, bond funds, and money market funds, but within those categories as well. Your mix of mutual funds should include diversifying across types of funds (money market, equities, and bonds), across time horizons (short-term, intermediate, and long-term bond funds), across industries (stock in telecommunications, health care, manufacturing, food, etc.), and across bond quality (government, corporate, municipal, and high-yield).

The nine asset allocation portfolios combine growth and in-come funds with maximum growth funds, and may add international equity funds too. To increase diversification, you could allocate your maximum growth fund investments between two funds, one of which invests for value, buying stocks of companies that are trading for less than the real value of their net assets, and one of which invests for traditional growth. Sometimes value-oriented funds do better than traditional growth funds, and some-times the reverse is true. By investing in both, you'll do well no matter which type is currently top dog.

You can increase your diversification among industries as well. If you buy a maximum growth fund that invests heavily in one indus-try, such as technology, consider investing in another fund that invests in a broader cross-section of industries.

To diversify the bond portion of your asset allocation, consider both intermediate and long-term bond funds. Intermediate bond funds are less volatile than long-term bond funds when interest rates are rising, and long-term bond funds perform better when interest rates ease off and begin to fall.

Also consider investing in both government and corporate bond funds. Government funds often yield a bit less than corpo-rate bond funds, but are less volatile and will retain their value better in uncertain economic times. Add a global bond fund to help cushion interest rate jitters caused by movement of the dollar against other currencies. If the economy is strong, you might also consider a high-yield (read "junk") bond fund com-prised of distressed or lower-rated bonds that pay higher interest rates and may skyrocket in value if the company recovers its financial health. If you are in a high tax bracket, the tax-free yield of a municipal bond fund may save you income taxes, unless your investment is already sheltered from taxes within a retirement plan.

Investing is like playing a guitar: you can make it as simple or as complex as you like, and still gain satisfactory results, if you stick with it. The important thing is to get started now. Find the right asset allocation portfolio for you, add a little extra diversification if you like, and then go to the next chapter to pick the right funds for you. "The biggest sin," says Florynce Kennedy, author and activist, "is sitting on your ass."

4
. . . .

STEP 3
Picking the
Right Funds for You

Now that you have identified the types of funds that are right for you and the percentage of your money to allocate to each, it's time to pick the particular funds in which you'll invest.

Before you begin, decide whether you will use a financial professional to help choose your investments, or invest on your own. This chapter will show you how to invest on your own. If you decide to use the services of a professional, turn to Chapter 11 to learn about load funds and how to choose the right financial professional.

Although there are over 5,200 funds from which to choose, it really isn't as difficult to pick mutual funds as it might seem. Of those 5,200 funds, nearly 1,000 are money market funds, so you only have to choose from among 4,200 funds for the bulk of your investments. If you use the services of a financial professional who sells securities, you will select from the broker-sold funds, which number about 2,700. These funds are generally front-load funds, which charge a sales commission when you purchase. If you invest on your own, you'll choose from no-load funds, which charge no sales commission, and low-loads, which carry a sales commission of 3 percent or less. This narrows your choices down to about 1,500 funds.

If your money is limited, and you are investing less than $1,000 in each fund, you will narrow your choices even more as you eliminate a large number of funds whose required minimum investments are greater than that.

This may still seem like a staggering number of funds from which to choose, but in reality, 1,500 funds aren't so many at all. Each week you choose from among far more food products than that at your local supermarket, and making those choices isn't overwhelming. Choosing mutual funds is not as complicated a process as you might have thought. Remember that 92 percent of your investment success comes from the way in which your assets are allocated, and you've already determined the best allocation for you. The rest is fairly easy: You must simply avoid the half of the funds that perform below average, and pick some solid performers from the rest. You don't have to pick the funds that will perform the best in the coming year. No one can predict that with certainty. Your goal is to pick funds that have weathered the investment storm year after year, and will continue to do so.

FUNDS REQUIRING LOW MINIMUM INVESTMENTS

Many no-load funds have higher minimum investment requirements than funds sold by stockbrokers. But most no-load funds require much lower minimum investments if you are investing IRA or SEP–IRA funds.

If you enroll in an automatic monthly investment plan, allowing the fund to draw a set amount from your checking or savings account each month, a number of mutual fund companies will waive their initial minimum investment requirement. Invesco, Neuberger & Berman, T. Rowe Price, Scudder, Strong, and Twentieth Century Investors, all of whom have a variety of funds, require no minimum if you invest $50 or more each month through an automatic investment plan. Smaller mutual fund companies with the same policy include Berger, Founders, Janus, Legg Mason, Portico, and WPG.

Value Line allows you to invest as little as $40 per month in its funds with no initial minimum investment, and PBHG will open your account for only $25 a month.

Loads, Fees, and Expenses

Front-Load Funds

When you purchase a fund through a stockbroker, it will likely be a front-load fund, which means that a sales commission, called a load, is included in the sales price. Those loads generally range from 4.5 to 8.5 percent. For example, if you invest $1,000 in a mutual fund with a front load of 5 percent, $50 of your investment will be taken for a sales commission, and your net investment in the fund will be only $950.

No-Load Funds

If you invest on your own, you will invest in mutual funds that sell their products directly to the public. For the most part, these funds are no-load funds, which means none of your money goes toward paying a sales commission, and 100 percent of the money you invest is put to work for you. No-load funds now account for over half the total assets in mutual funds, including money market funds.

Low-Load Funds

Some fund families such as Fidelity have added loads of 3 percent or so to new funds and funds that were previously sold no-load. But having met with some resistance to that practice, Fidelity now waives its loads on most funds purchased for retirement accounts. Other low-load funds periodically have "specials" during which no load is charged, or let investors in a new fund invest free of load, although loads will be charged to subsequent investors.

Slow-Load Funds

Some funds charge small annual fees which I call "slow-load." These 12b-1 fees, named after the 1980 Securities and Exchange Commission rule that permits them, cover distribution costs, a fancy term for the cost of advertising and selling the fund to you.

At least half of all funds levy some sort of 12b-1 fee. The fee cannot be higher than .75 percent of assets per year, plus an additional .25 percent service fee, for a total of 1 percent. Funds charging 12b-1 fees can't call themselves no-load unless the fee is .25 percent or less.

The fee may not seem like much, but it is charged each year on the fund value, so it goes up as the value of your fund grows. When the 12b-1 fee was first introduced, it could be imposed year after year; after a number of years the aggregate 12b-1 fee might amount to far more than the greatest front load. Under new rules an investor cannot pay more than an aggregate of 8.5 percent in 12b-1 fees for each fund. Some funds cap the 12b-1 fee at an aggregate of 3 or 4 percent.

Freeload

If you invest in a family of funds that charges a load, you may be allowed to switch from one fund to another without additional charge. This is called freeloading, and generally applies if you buy a fund within ninety days of selling another fund within the same family.

Don't Be Naive About NAV

For front-load funds, the load is included in the price of the fund. Funds are priced each day by computing the net asset value per share, known as the NAV, and then adding the load to the NAV. That becomes the "offer price," which you must pay to buy the fund. When you sell the fund, however, all you will receive is the NAV. For no-load funds, the NAV and the offer price are the same, because there is no markup for load.

Other Fees

Be alert to other fees charged by no-load funds. Some funds charge a redemption fee when the shares are sold (a fee that sometimes disappears after a year) or a transaction fee when the shares are purchased. These fees are paid to the fund itself, and merely pass along to the individual investor the transaction costs of investing or liquidating his or her shares. Because these fees are paid to the fund (that is, to the existing shareholders), the fees are equitable and should not be viewed in the same light as loads, which are paid to a sales force and not to the fund itself.

The Vanguard Group, one of the largest mutual fund companies, now charges a small transaction fee on its index funds to cover the transaction costs of investing the money, and a small quarterly maintenance fee besides. These fees are payable to the fund, not to an adviser or sales organization, and they compensate existing shareholders for the costs the fund incurs to invest the money brought in by new shareholders.

Expenses

All mutual funds charge operating expenses and management fees, which are deducted from the total return you receive each year. These expenses include the investment advisory fee or management fee, which ranges from .3 to 1 percent of fund assets, administrative costs, which are .2 to .5 percent, and other operating expenses of .1 to .4 percent. Added together, those combined fees range from .6 to 1.9 percent.

The fee table near the front of a fund's prospectus lists the annual expense ratios for recent years. The annual expense ratio is the fund's operating expenses, including management fees, 12b-1 fees (if any), and other expenses, divided by the fund's net assets. Obviously, the lower the expense ratio, the better, as expenses reduce the annual performance of the fund. Just because the fund's total return quoted in publications has those expenses already subtracted, don't think they don't matter. In a down year, when profits range from slim to none, a low annual expense ratio can mean the difference between making a small profit or losing money.

The funds offered by the Vanguard Group have, by far, the lowest costs, because the funds own the management company, so management and administrative services are provided at cost, reducing those charges considerably.

Choosing the Right Funds for You

There are a great number of good funds in every category on the market. Because 92 percent of your investment success will come

---

AVERAGE EXPENSE RATIOS

Here are the average expense ratios for various types of funds:

Aggressive growth stock	1.83%
Long-term growth stock	1.17
Growth and income stock	1.09
International and global	1.48
High-yield corporate bonds	.96
Corporate bonds	.70
Municipal bonds	.63
Government bonds	.71
Global bonds	1.06
Money market funds	.58

These figures do not include load, redemption, and 12b-1 fees.

---

from proper asset allocation, and only 8 percent depends on picking the right funds, don't worry about finding this year's absolute top performer. Look for funds with consistent performance histories that will yield solid returns year after year.

Where to Begin Your Search
You'll find reports on fund performance in a variety of financial publications. Each week *The Wall Street Journal* shows total returns for periods ranging from four weeks to five years. Comprehensive reports are published quarterly, semiannually, or annually by *Barron's, BusinessWeek, Financial Weekly, Forbes, Fortune, Kiplinger's Personal Finance, Money, Mutual Funds Magazine, Smart Money, U.S. News & World Report, Worth,* and others.

Mutual fund reports generally list funds by objective, grading the funds and showing the one-year, three-year, and ten-year performance of each fund. Most reports also note the sales charge (load) and latest annual expense ratio.

Investing in Fund Families

Consider keeping your money all in the family—or at least in a family or two. It's easy to do. The twenty largest fund families offer a combined total of over eight hundred different mutual funds. Large no-load and low-load fund families include Dreyfus, Fidelity, Gabelli, Janus, T. Rowe Price, Scudder, Twentieth Century Investors, and Vanguard. Large-load families include American Funds, Dean Witter, Franklin Funds, Kemper, Merrill Lynch, Paine Webber, and Putnam.

There are many advantages for investing in a single family of funds. Your transaction statements will be in a consistent format, and some funds even combine your funds onto a single account statement. You will be able to switch money from fund to fund with ease as your investment needs change. And if you are investing in funds that charge a load, the load may be reduced if you invest a certain amount within the same family of funds. The breakpoints for load reductions are clearly spelled out in the prospectus.

Some advisers counsel against investing within a single family of funds, arguing that a fund company's philosophy will cause its funds to be too much alike, and thus diminish the benefits of diversification. However, in actuality that is rarely true, because different fund managers striving to meet different fund goals rarely invest alike. Occasionally, a family of funds will contain several funds with the same general goal (growth, maximum growth, income, etc.) and with the same manager, and those funds do tend to invest alike. Because of the similarity, if you invest within the same family you should buy shares in one or the other of such similar funds, but not both.

Of course, if a single family of funds doesn't offer all the funds you need, or excels in only some of the fund categories you need, you will want to expand your investments to more than one fund family.

Stand-Alone Funds

You may be attracted to a fund that is part of a very small family of funds or even a single stand-alone fund. Do consider such a fund if you are a buy-and-hold investor who won't be switching your money from fund to fund frequently, and if you don't mind the inconvenience of multiple statements and tax-reporting forms. If the fund is successful, it may even become the centerpiece around which a family of funds grows. Many fund families have begun this way.

SAFETY OF YOUR FUND

When choosing a family of funds, concentrate on performance and service, not the safety of your money. Even if the funds' sponsor has financial difficulty, your money won't disappear, as the fund assets are insulated from claims of the sponsor's creditors. Nor can the fund manager run off with your money: the Investment Company Act of 1940 requires that all officers with access to money be covered by fidelity bond coverage. And the Securities Investor Protection Corporation (SIPC), which is much like the FDIC for banks, guarantees that your mutual fund shares will be safe even if a brokerage firm holding them for you goes bankrupt.

Using Magazine Mutual Fund Reports

Here's how to use the mutual fund performance reports that appear in magazines.

First, turn to the section that discusses top-performing funds in the categories that apply to you. Are there any family names that appear in several categories? Although it isn't absolutely necessary to invest within the same family, it does make searching for funds more convenient.

Review the listings for funds that are no-load or low-load to find several highly rated funds within each fund category of your investment portfolio (see Chapter 3). Pick several funds that appeal to you in each category.

If you are investing less than $1,000 in each category, but you plan to make monthly investments, refer to the list on page 44 of mutual funds that waive minimums if you agree to make automatic monthly investments. If you do not plan to make monthly investments, call the fund's 800 number to ask about the required minimum investment. (If your library subscribes to Morningstar or another rating service, you'll find the information regarding minimum investments there as well.) Several of your choices may be eliminated because their required minimum investment is too high for your investment resources.

Using Morningstar, Value Line, and Other Rating Services

You may use Morningstar's reports, or those of another rating service, to look for funds. Look at funds that have three-, four-, and five-star ratings, and select several strong performers. Look at the total return section, comparing the best and worst years over a ten-year period to the S&P 500 stock index.

Fund Comparison Worksheet

Once you have found several funds in each category that appeal to you, fill out Worksheet 4.1 using data from the fund listings:

WORKSHEET 4.1

	Fund A	Fund B	Fund C
Name of fund			
800 number			
Total return:			
1-year performance			
3-year performance			
5-year performance			
10-year performance			
Load			
Last year's expense ratio			
Minimum investment:			
IRA			
Initial			
Automatic investment plan			

When comparing performance, always compare funds to other funds of the same type and to benchmark indexes. Although good performance over the past one, three, five, or ten years does not guarantee good future performance, it does indicate the quality of management. Avoid funds that have consistently performed poorly for several years. Studies show that those funds are likely to continue their trend of poor performance into the future.

Now pick two or three of the funds, call the 800 number that appears in the listing, and request a prospectus. If you like several funds of a particular fund family, request prospectuses for as many of the funds in that group as you might use.

Fund Advertising

As you leaf through the financial publications that come your way, you will find advertisements for mutual funds that tout their performance. "Best fund in its class for three years in a row," the ad might say. But what the ad doesn't tell you is that it defined its "class" so narrowly that it couldn't miss being number one. For example, the class a growth fund has carved out for its advertisement may not be growth funds in general, but rather "growth funds sold by our mutual fund company." Or perhaps the deception lies in the part of the ad that tells you it's been the best fund "for three years in a row." Perhaps those three years were 1984 through 1986, and its performance has been mediocre ever since. New SEC guidelines should cure any deceptive advertising. Now when funds cite their performance rankings, they must provide details on how the rankings were formulated, and for what period.

Quality of Service

Although you won't deal with the mutual fund company every day, you want good service when you do. Service includes telephone responses, mailed statements and shareholder reports, and the types of amenities offered by the company. Here are some of the services that you might find important:

An 800 number. Does the fund offer an 800 number? If not, you will have to pay for a long-distance call each time to contact them. That will be particularly expensive if their operators are all busy and you are put on hold.

Hours of telephone service. Many fund companies offer twenty-four-hour telephone service, but others limit service to as little as standard business hours, Monday through Friday. If that fits your schedule in your time zone, fine. If not, choose a company that will talk to you when it's convenient for you.

Telephone switching. If you decide to switch from one fund to another, will your fund let you do so by telephone, or must you notify them by letter?

Telephone redemption. When you want to redeem all or a portion of your investment, can you do so by telephone? Some funds require a letter for all transactions or for transactions over a certain amount, and some require a letter with a signature guaranteed by your stockbroker or bank. Those letters and signature guarantees can be a royal pain in the neck when you are trying to access your money fast.

Wire transfers. When you redeem your shares, can the money be wired directly to the bank, or must you wait several days until the company issues a check, mails it to you, and the post office delivers it?

Automatic investment plans. Many funds allow you to make monthly investments automatically. The mutual fund company will draw funds from your bank account monthly or quarterly through an electronic draft, and those funds will be invested in the fund. This plan is a real boon for procrastinators. (Wouldn't it be great if health clubs would follow the mutual fund's lead and offer an automatic exercise plan?)

Minimum initial investment and subsequent investments. If you are starting small, choose a mutual fund company that will allow small initial investments augmented by small monthly investments. Some companies will waive their initial investment requirement completely if you enroll in their automatic investment plan.

Number of free exchanges. Many mutual fund companies offer unlimited exchanges from one fund to another within the company, but others allow only a few a year. If you don't plan to switch often, that won't be a problem for you. As a matter of fact, because frequent switches increase the fund's expenses for transaction costs and paperwork processing, you may prefer funds that limit the number of exchanges and thus keep their costs down. Remember, fund expenses are deducted from the return the fund pays you.

Check-writing privileges. You can write checks on almost all money market funds, but the checks generally must exceed a minimum amount, such as $500, and many funds charge a small fee for each check written. A few short-term bond funds allow you check-writing privileges as well, but they can complicate your tax return. Money market funds are always valued at $1 per share, so redemptions from such funds don't have to be reported on your tax return. But checks written on other funds, such as short-term bond funds, are actually share redemptions, so each check you write will be reported on your tax return as a sale, complicating your return and increasing preparation time and costs.

TELEPHONE SERVICE

When you call the mutual fund company's 800 number, you will be able to assess the quality of telephone service to investors. If the mutual fund company doesn't have an 800 number, let that be the first clue as to how the company feels about you. Ask questions about how you should decide among the company's stock funds, and what the average maturity is in the various bond funds. Don't be afraid to let your ignorance show. Ask tough questions, or ask stupid questions—either way, you will get a feel for the knowledge and courtesy of the fund's staff.

Derivatives

Some bond funds got clobbered in 1994, as did the Orange County, California, treasury, when interest rates climbed, because they were holding volatile derivatives. Derivatives are any security that derives its value from another security. Because derivatives are zero-sum, they have no underlying economic value, so if one investor wins, another one loses, as in poker. The money is always there, but the pockets change. That makes derivatives an extremely volatile gamble. Derivatives are designed to enhance return in steady markets, but they turned into exploding time bombs when interest rates ticked up. To find out if a bond fund has a large amount of derivatives, here's what to do:

Call the 800 number for the fund and ask them. The fund representative should be able to tell you what types of derivatives are held and what percentage of the portfolio they comprise.

Research it yourself. Though the information isn't in the prospectus, you can look at the list of the fund's holdings in the quarterly or semiannual report for words such as collateralized mortgage obligations (CMOs), inverse floaters, interest only (I/O), principal only (P/O), indexed securities, mortgage strips, structured notes, and tranche. Add up all the holdings identified by these words, then divide by the total fund holdings. If the derivatives are more than 10 percent of the total holdings, the fund is taking a great deal of added risk to enhance returns. If you don't want to take those risks, choose a different fund.

Performance Results—What Do They Mean?

To pick the right mutual fund, consider performance first. Look at one-year, three-year, five-year, and ten-year performance. A study of mutual fund performance for twenty consecutive years showed that the fund with the top average any given five-year period did not do nearly so well in the next five years. That is because market cycles generally are two to four years long, so it is not likely that the cycle of the past five years will be repeated during the next five years. As economic conditions change and funds move into and out of sync with the market, you will definitely find that long-term past performance does not accurately predict future short-term performance. But don't pick mutual funds based on a great one-year performance, either. A study by John Bogle, chief at the Vanguard Group, reports that the top-ranked equity fund for each of the ten years ending in 1992 had an average rank of 100 (out of 681) in the next year.

Don't be carried away by today's hot performer. When considering past performance, pick funds that have done well in both up and down markets for a number of years, and stick with them. A well-run fund should perform well, on average, for years and years.

How Many Funds Should You Own?

If you are investing $10,000 or less, choose just one fund in each of the fund categories. If you are investing more than that, you may choose an additional fund or two in each category, though it really isn't necessary. It is not important to hold a number of different funds in each category, as it would be if you were holding individual stocks. Investing in two funds that are similar will not diminish risk. Diversification among types of funds does decrease risk, because of the offsetting patterns of return among the investments. But this is true only if the portfolio has diverse components, and investing in two funds of similar type does not produce this diversity.

Some investors buy the hot performers each year, but never sell any of their prior fund investments. After several years, they have a complicated mishmash of overlapping funds that are difficult to monitor. Some are performing well, and some enjoyed only a brief time in the spotlight before they faded. These investors own funds just as some people eat berries: they begin by choosing only the best, and end up eating everything. To keep this from happening to you, here are some rules to follow:

Stick to your asset allocation. If you find a new fund you want to buy, make sure it fits your portfolio's objectives.

Limit the number of funds you own. That way, you will be forced to weed out the poor performers before you invest in a new fund.

Don't let your investments overwhelm you. If you find you own more funds than you can handle, combine your investments in similar funds until you have weeded your investment garden to a manageable few funds. If necessary, make an asset allocation fund your core investment, letting the fund manager allocate your money among stocks, bonds, and cash. You can supplement that core investment with an extra fund or two to add other dimensions you might need, such as international equity funds.

Picking the Right Money Market Fund

Money market funds invest in short-term securities issued by financial and governmental institutions, generally with maturities of ninety days or less. Money market funds always trade at par, so the value of your principal remains constant—every dollar you invest is always worth exactly one dollar—and the interest rate you receive fluctuates daily. You can redeem your investment at any time, and many funds provide check-writing privileges. The earnings of most money market funds are taxable, although you can also purchase tax-exempt money market funds that invest only in short-term municipal bonds. Money market funds often pay higher interest than checking or savings accounts, and are an ideal parking place for money you are saving for a special purchase, irregular expenses, or a vacation.

When choosing a money market fund, be aware of the minimum investment required, the minimum size of check you can write, and any fees charged for check writing and account maintenance. Consider the fund's yield in comparison to that of other funds: generally, the lower the fund's expenses, the higher the yield, so look at expenses too. The average expense is about .75 percent, but many funds are well below that.

Consider the type of securities in which the money market fund invests—if you are in a high tax bracket you may want tax-exempt income, or you may prefer the extra security of a money market fund that invests only in U.S. government securities. Remember that money market funds carry no FDIC insurance as do bank savings and checking accounts. No one has ever lost money in a money market fund, but a couple of funds have teetered on the brink. For safety, choose a fund whose average maturity is no longer than the average for all taxable funds. Most major newspapers publish the current average maturities and yields for all major money market funds.

Convenience is important, too. If you invest through a stockbroker, you'll probably want to have a money market account that is tied to your brokerage account, so it can receive the proceeds from sales and dividends, and so you can put money there in anticipation of future investments. If you do your own investing, you may want to park your cash in the money market fund of one of the fund families in which you invest.

MONEY MARKET FUND FEATURES

To decide which fund is best for you, decide which features are most important:

• If you plan to use the fund as a checking account, pay attention to those that have no check charges and low minimum check amounts.

• If you are using it as a savings account, look for highest yields.

• If you have little to invest, look for funds with low minimum investments.

• If you are concerned with safety or tax benefits, look for funds that invest in government securities or mutual bonds.

Buying Mutual Fund Shares

To open an account, either as a direct investment or with a broker, you will need to provide some basic information: the name you would like on the account; your address, age, and Social Security number; whether you want to receive the dividends from the fund or reinvest them; whether you want to provide for telephone transfers or redemptions or check writing; and whether you want to set up an automatic deposit from your checking or savings account.

When you register your mutual funds, it will be as an individual, as tenants in common with someone else, or as a joint tenant with someone else. If you register as a joint tenant, the surviving tenant will inherit the account if you die, regardless of what your will says. Income taxes on the earnings of the account will be paid by the person who owns the funds that went into the account. For example, if you invest your own money in an account, the earnings will be taxable to you alone, regardless of whether you own the account individually or as a joint tenant or tenant in common with someone else. But if you and a friend each invest equally in an account, the earnings will be taxed one-half to each of you.

After you have invested in the mutual fund, you will generally receive statements every time there is a transaction (purchase, redemption, or dividend reinvestment) to be reported, and you'll receive a summary statement at the end of the year. You will also receive annual reports and other shareholder information. Some fund families even publish a regular newsletter that goes to all shareholders.

Selling your shares in a mutual fund is as easy as dialing a phone, if you have arranged for telephone redemption. If your fund does not allow for telephone redemption, read the shareholder services section of the fund prospectus to see what procedure must be followed to redeem shares. Some funds require a letter of intent instructing them as to what to do with your fund shares, which must have a signature guarantee from a commercial bank or a stockbroker. If this is too cumbersome a process for you, you may want to stick with funds that allow for telephone redemption.

Buying Through Discount Brokers

Discount brokers have begun to offer funds from a variety of different fund families, but the discount broker will not give you advice on which funds to choose. The advantage of dealing with a discount broker is convenience: you are able to buy funds of several companies with one phone call, and your funds can be kept all in one account. You can acquire mutual fund shares through discount brokers such as Charles Schwab, Jack White, and Fidelity Investments without additional transaction fees. Each of these brokers offers more than two hundred different funds from several families, with more added regularly. For the buy-and-hold investor who wants a greater selection, discount brokers won't be of any great benefit. But for the investor who wants to move money from fund to fund and family to family frequently, discount brokers immensely ease the way.

If you buy mutual funds through discount brokers for your retirement account, you can avoid the multiple custodial fees that would be charged if you had retirement accounts with several different funds.

By investing through a discount broker you can sometimes invest smaller amounts than the fund's minimum requirement. Buying through a discount broker will also allow you to buy on margin, borrowing against the mutual funds you hold in your account. One discount broker, Jack White & Co., offers a service whereby you can buy a load fund for a flat $200 fee, rather than pay a percentage load to purchase the fund. The service is called CONNECT, and the trade is made by placing your offer on an electronic bulletin board and waiting for a seller to respond. There is, of course, no guarantee that a willing seller can be found right away, so the trade may not take place the day you place your order.

When to Buy Mutual Funds

In general, the best time to buy mutual funds is when you have the money. Don't wait for the market to drop—you have no way of knowing. But there are some things you can do to improve your fund performance, no matter when you invest.

Buy or sell late in the day. Mutual funds are bought and sold at the price as of the close of business on the trading day. For that reason, if you are trying to time your investment for best advantage, you might as well wait until three o'clock eastern time to make your decision, because you will have a better idea of where the market might close at four. Otherwise, if you see the market dip in the morning and decide to buy, you may be disappointed if it makes a full recovery in the afternoon, and your purchase price is much higher than you wanted.

Pay attention to dividends. Avoid buying a mutual fund just before a dividend distribution, unless you are investing for an IRA or SEP–IRA (Simplified Employee Pension Plan) account. Upon dividend distribution, the price of the fund will drop by the amount of the dividend. If you buy just before the dividend, you will pay more for the shares, and the dividend will be taxable to you when you receive it. If you wait until after the dividend is paid, the share price will be lower and you will not receive taxable income. Most stock funds distribute the biggest dividends in December. Call the toll-free number for the fund to find out the next distribution date.

Buy early in a recovery. If you want to time the market, buy when you can see enough to know there must be light at the end of the recession tunnel. Don't wait until you are well into the daylight of recovery. By that time, the savvy investor will be anticipating the next tunnel.

Invest gradually. If you are investing a lump sum, ease yourself into the fund. Invest 20 percent now, and 20 percent more at the end of each quarter. By the end of the year, you will be fully invested, and you will have avoided the risk of buying just before the market takes a tumble. If the market drops after your initial investment, you will acquire more shares when you make the subsequent investments. (*Caution:* At the beginning of a rising market, this may not be the best strategy, since you'll miss growth opportunity by the delay. Try investing over a shorter period of time, say, 20 percent now and 20 percent at the end of each month, so that you become fully invested in four months rather than a year.)

5
• • • • • • • •

READING THE PROSPECTUS
What to Look For

R emember when you were told to eat your carrots because they are good for your eyes? Just as carrots improve your eyesight, reading a mutual fund prospectus will improve your financial viewpoint. The prospectus is a twenty- to thirty-page booklet that discusses the fund's history, investment objectives, performance, and management, and gives the essential facts you need to make an intelligent decision. Unfortunately, like all factual tomes, the mutual fund prospectus can seem impenetrable. It is a legal document, often printed on tissue-like white paper, and the printing and language are often quite dense. But don't despair: the prospectus is short, so there aren't many pages to read, and you don't have to read every word, only the highlights.

The Securities and Exchange Commission requires that you receive a copy of the prospectus before you invest, but no law requires you to read the prospectus. Because of the formidable appearance of the prospectus, many investors don't read it. You should.

Many mutual fund companies have improved the layout and readability of their prospectuses in recent years. Newer versions are often two-color, with larger type, and charts and headlines that help guide you through the maze of information. Though still densely packed with data, they are no longer impenetrable.

Someday soon the SEC is expected to approve a "summary prospectus" that is just one page long, so that mutual funds will even be able to print the summaries in their ads. The new one-page prospectus will contain twenty bits of information, including investment objective, historical returns, fees, expenses, and risk. If you want more information, the longer prospectus will still be available.

Highlights of the Prospectus

When you request information about funds, the mutual fund company will send you a prospectus for each fund. Open the prospectus to the beginning. Toward the front you will find the portions that discuss investment objectives, investment policies, risks, costs, and the ten-year per share data table. Now turn to the back of the prospectus to find information about shareholder services. As you scan the data at the front and at the back of the prospectus, answer these questions:

Does This Fund Fit My Goals?

Read the short investment objective at the beginning of the prospectus very carefully, to make sure it meshes with your needs. It may not fit your investor profile. For example, if your asset mix calls for a growth and income fund, don't buy an aggressive growth fund just because it's had high returns in recent years. Instead, search out a growth and income fund that stands out among similar funds.

The Investment Company Institute, which is the trade organization for mutual funds, has prepared a booklet called "An Investor's Guide to Reading the Mutual Fund Prospectus," which it will be happy to send to you. You can order a free copy from the institute at 1600 M Street NW, Suite 600, Washington, D.C. 20036. In the booklet, the ICI has compiled a list of typical statements of investment objectives. Here are some examples:

• *Aggressive growth fund:* "The investment objective of the fund is long-term capital appreciation. The generation of current income is only a secondary objective."

- *Global equity fund:* "The fund's investment objective is to earn a high level of total return through investments in the various capital markets of the world."
- *Balanced fund:* "The fund strives for the balanced accomplishment of three investment objectives—income, capital growth, and stability."
- *Municipal bond fund:* "The fund's investment objective is to seek as high a level of interest income exempt from federal income tax as is consistent with the preservation of capital."

Can I Afford the Minimum Required to Purchase This Fund?
Now read the minimum investment required in the section titled "How to Purchase Shares." Many funds require minimum investments of $2,500 or so, and some require $25,000 or more. If the minimum investment is out of your range, the fund isn't for you. Send for prospectuses for some of the funds of mutual fund families that let you start with $50 to $1,000. See Chapter 4 for a listing of some of those funds.

What Latitude Does the Fund Manager Have?
Look at the section of the prospectus called "Investment Techniques," "Investment Principles," or something similar. This section tells the lengths to which the fund manager is allowed to go to enhance return, and how far he or she can retreat to prevent losses. Borrowing money can enhance a fund's performance in a bull market, but it may be dangerous if the market turns. If you don't like to borrow money, you won't want to invest in a fund that has the latitude to *leverage* (borrow money to invest). Other words that signal added risk are *naked options* and *hedging*, which refer to techniques that allow equity funds to bet which way the market will go without purchasing shares of the stock itself; and *high-yield*, which describes bonds of lower credit grade, with considerable risk of principal, otherwise known as "junk." It's okay to invest in funds that use these strategies, but understand that they are taking on more risk in pursuit of greater reward. Most funds allow managers to invest some or all of the fund's assets in short-term or cash

securities if they fear a market drop. If you want a fund that bails out of the stock market if it sees trouble on the horizon, don't invest in one that is required to stay fully invested at all times. Read this section of the prospectus carefully to learn the policy of the fund.

What Is the Annual Total Return?

Total return is a combination of dividends from net income, dividends from capital gains, and the net increase (or decrease) in the value of the stocks or bonds in the portfolio (net asset value). You can compute total return for the year by adding together these three components and dividing by the net asset value at the beginning of the year. You will find this data in the per-share table, and also in the tables of fund performance in financial magazines and other publications. Compare the fund's track record for each year to that of similar funds, and also to a benchmark index. Look for a fund that does well in down markets as well as up markets.

DOW JONES AND FRIENDS

Most people have heard of the Dow Jones Industrial Average, a composite of thirty stocks, because that is the number that is reported on the TV news each evening. But with over two thousand different issues on the New York Stock Exchange alone, not to mention the American Stock Exchange and the over-the-counter market, how can a composite of thirty stocks be representative of the stock market? It can't. Still, the Dow Jones Industrial Average is worth watching simply because everyone else watches it, and overall market movement has a great deal to do with investor sentiment. A more accurate indicator to watch for overall market movement is the Standard & Poor's 500 stock index for larger-cap stocks, which comprise about 70 percent of the total U.S. stock market value. To gauge performance of the other 30 percent of the stock market, look at the Wilshire 4500 index. Small-company performance is indicated by the Russell 2000 small stock index. Foreign equity performance appears in the Morgan Stanley EAFE index, and bond performance is tracked by the Lehman Brothers Aggregate.

BENCHMARK INDEXES

Here are the benchmark indexes that you can use to compare the total return of funds you are considering to the performance of the market as a whole:

- Growth funds: Wilshire 4500 (small and medium stocks)
- Aggressive growth funds: Russell 2000 (small stocks)
- Growth and income funds: S&P 500 (large "blue-chip" stocks)
- Bonds: Lehman Brothers Aggregate

TABLE 5.1

BENCHMARK INDEXES—TOTAL RETURN

Year	Large Stocks S&P 500	Small to Medium Stocks Wilshire 4500	Small Stocks Russell 2000	Int'l Stocks EAFE	Bonds LB Aggregate
1994	1.31	−2.65	−1.82	7.78	−2.92
1993	10.06	14.53	18.90	32.56	9.75
1992	7.62	11.75	18.41	−12.17	7.25
1991	30.48	43.45	46.05	12.13	16.00
1990	−3.12	−13.56	−19.51	−23.45	8.95
1989	31.68	23.94	16.24	10.53	14.54
1988	16.62	20.53	24.89	28.27	7.88
1987	5.26	−3.51	−8.77	24.63	2.75
1986	18.68	11.76	5.68	69.44	15.25
1985	31.74	32.02	31.06	56.16	22.13
1984	6.26	−1.72	−7.30	7.38	15.16

How Much Are the Fees?

You'll find these near the beginning of the prospectus, in a section called "Fee Table" or "Fund Expenses." Look for front-load fees, which you are charged when you buy shares in the fund; redemption fees, which you are charged when you sell shares in the fund;

and 12b-1 fees, which you are charged each year you own shares in the fund. If you are buying a load fund, there may be reduced sales charges for larger share purchases, depending on how much you invest. For example, the breakpoints might be: 4 percent fee for purchases less than $10,000, 3 percent for purchases of $10,000 to $50,000, 2 percent for purchases of $50,000 to $100,000, 1 percent for purchases of $100,000 to $250,000, and no load for purchases of $250,000 or more.

If the fund charges a front load, this section of the prospectus will tell you whether the fund family will allow you to move money from one fund to another without paying an additional load. This is a valuable benefit, as it allows you to transfer your money from a fund that is performing poorly, or whose investment objectives no longer match your own, into a fund more suited to your needs— without paying additional costs.

What Are the Expenses?
The per-share table shows the ratio of total expenses to average net assets. The lower the number, the lower the expenses. When comparing expenses, don't assume that funds with lower expenses will perform better than funds with higher expenses. Small funds generally have higher expense ratios than large ones, but they may be more nimble at getting in and out of investments, as they are able to buy or sell shares in smaller quantities and thus not affect the price of the shares when they buy or sell. For this reason, they may offer higher returns than the larger, more cumbersome funds, which can leave a volatile wake as they propel their way through the financial waters. Funds requiring smaller minimum investments often have higher expenses, because smaller average account sizes have higher shareholder-servicing costs. Global and international funds tend to have higher expense ratios than domestic portfolios, and stock funds have higher expense ratios than bond funds. When comparing expense ratios among funds, compare the ratios of similar types of funds to each other rather than to those of other types of funds. If the fund is new, the footnotes will tell you if the fees and costs are being subsidized. That's a boon to fund

performance now, but be aware that the policy won't last forever, so you need to know what the full costs will be after the subsidy ends.

What Are the Risks?

Read the risk section and any other warnings that appear in red letters, capitals, or bold-faced sections. These are the "How I can lose money" clauses, and warn of risky investment practices, impending lawsuits, and changes in fees or investment practices. If you don't understand the language, call shareholder services and ask them for clarification.

Does the Fund Offer the Services I Require?

Look at the section on shareholder services in the back of the prospectus. Does the fund offer reinvestment of dividends and capital gains without fees or loads? Can you move money between funds or redeem your shares by telephone? If the fund is a money market fund or a short-term bond fund, does it offer check-writing privileges? Does the fund offer an accumulation plan, waiving the initial minimum investment in the fund in exchange for regular investments? Will the fund arrange for direct deposit from your bank? How do you get your money out? Does the fund offer telephone switch and telephone redemption services? Are telephone redemptions limited to a ceiling amount? If so, what is the procedure for greater redemptions? Will your signature need to be guaranteed? Are wire transfers allowed? Make sure the funds you are considering offer the conveniences you want. A word of caution: Sometimes conveniences such as telephone transfer are available for some funds within a family and not for others. If you have any questions, just pick up the telephone and call shareholder services. They should be able to answer your question right away.

If you plan to invest additional money on a regular basis, make sure the fund offers an automatic investment plan through which it draws money regularly from your checking account. If you want instant access to your money, make sure your fund provides for telephone exchange and wire transfers. Ask shareholder services how soon the fund will send your check after you telephone them with a redemption request. Although Securities and Exchange Commission regulations allow them one week to mail the check to you, many funds do so the next day.

The Per-Share Table

Now review in detail the per-share table for the funds that have passed muster. The per-share table, which contains fund data for the past ten years, is one of the most useful parts of the prospectus. An updated per-share table is also included in the annual shareholder reports.

The per-share table contains information regarding investment income, expenses, dividends, capital gains distributions, increases or decreases in the fund value during the year, expense ratios, portfolio turnover rate, and number of shares outstanding.

Look at the specific performance of the fund for *each* of the years, compared to that of other funds of the same type, and compared to the major stock market indexes or index funds. You want a fund that is a consistent performer from year to year. Funds that have erratic records may give you more of a roller-coaster ride than you can stomach, particularly those funds that fare badly in bear markets.

Funds with a higher income ratio pay regular dividends, and they tend to be more stable than those with little or no income, but remember that the dividends are taxable to you each year. Capital gains are taxable only when the underlying stock is sold and the gain is actually realized, so it may be years before you pay tax on much of the increased value of a profitable fund.

What to Look for in a Fund

When picking a fund, the most important things to consider are past performance, expenses, management, portfolio turnover, and risk. These are all spelled out in the prospectus, and the information is also included in reports issued by rating services such as Morningstar and Value Line as well as in some rating reports in financial magazines.

If your investment time horizon is less than ten years, you'll be better off with a slightly lower return from a fund that takes fewer risks, rather than with a somewhat higher return from a fund that takes lots of risks. But if your time horizon is long, you can weather the volatility of a risky fund. Otherwise, look for stability when you analyze past performance by looking at the year-by-year results in addition to the average performance over a three-, five-, or ten-year period.

If you are investing for a long haul, the up-front load is of relatively little consequence compared to annual expenses and 12b-1 fees. If you frequently shift your money from fund to fund, you will find a fund that charges an annual 12b-1 fee to be less expensive than one with a front load or a substantial exit fee, which will be incurred each time you move your money.

When shopping for bond funds, look at the average maturity of the fund's portfolio: a lower average maturity means the bonds will mature in the next few years, and so the fund will have lower price volatility. A lower average maturity may also result in lower returns when interest rates fall, so if interest rates are reaching their zenith, you may prefer a higher average maturity.

Also look at the bond fund's standard deviation in performance, which is the margin of error. A standard deviation of 3 tells you that two-thirds of the time a bond fund may swing 3 percentage points over or below its average return for the year. For example, if the fund averages 7 percent for the year with a standard deviation of 3, chances are its earnings will be somewhere between 4 and 10 percent. One-third of the time the returns are likely to be above or below that range. If you cannot tolerate that much volatility, a lower average maturity coupled with a higher-quality bond, such as U.S. Treasury or agency bonds, should lower the standard deviation. Unfortunately, it will probably lower the average return as well.

Portfolio Turnover Rate

To compute portfolio turnover rate, the value of assets that a fund has purchased or sold over the course of a year is divided by the fund's net assets. It shows the amount of buying and selling that the fund does. A 100 percent turnover implies that each stock or bond is held an average of one year. A 50 percent turnover implies that each security is held for an average of two years. A 200 percent turnover shows an average holding period of only six months. In general, the lower the turnover ratio, the lower the transaction costs of buying and selling, and the less the taxable income from realized capital gains. When comparing the turnover rates for similar types of funds, look for portfolios with turnover ratios below 60 percent.

Fund Size

Fund size can also be important. Funds under $100 million are small, while funds over $500 million are large. All things being equal, look for smaller funds when investing in stock funds. They are better able to buy a company's stock quickly at opportune times, and sell a company's stock at the first sign of trouble without affecting stock prices. Larger funds have to sell stock gradually to avoid impacting the price. Small funds can hold fewer stocks, which means more concentrated holdings of those stocks that managers think are winners. A really large portfolio will have trouble beating the market because it holds such a large selection of stocks. But large portfolios do have some advantages, such as lower expense ratios. Large funds can also attract and better compensate prestigious managers.

Cash Flow

Cash flow, which is the net new money invested in a mutual fund, may also be significant. Look at the "ratios" section of the per-share table. You will find a line that tells you either the number of shares outstanding at the end of each year, or the net assets at the end of each year. If those numbers increase from one year to the next, investors have bought more shares than they have sold, pumping more cash into the fund and increasing its assets. If the number of shares dwindles from year to year, investors are bailing out faster than new investors are coming aboard, causing cash to flow out and net assets to drop.

A large inflow of cash has many advantages. It allows a fund manager to buy more shares of stocks the fund already holds, which may boost the value of the stock. The fund manager can also purchase shares in a company without having to sell a winning existing position in another stock. And the manager can amass cash to be invested if stocks decline, or to satisfy shareholder redemptions in a bear market without having to sell stocks that have declined.

But excess cash flow can also spell problems for a fund. As the market moves toward its peak, investors tend to pour money into funds, which may force the manager to invest when prices are high and likely to decline. If the manager chooses instead to keep the cash on hand, that cash will earn a low rate of interest, so a significant influx of new cash will result in an increasing portion of the portfolio invested at a low return. That will lower the average return on the portfolio as a whole.

Beware of negative cash flow, as it warns of possible inherent problems the fund is having. When cash flow is negative, net assets and outstanding shares decline. That means that investors are redeeming shares faster than new money is flowing in. That is happening for a reason: shareholders are unhappy with performance, the imposition of new fees, change in management, or some other reason. You can peg a negative cash flow by looking at the per-share table to see if there is a declining trend of shares outstanding or net assets at year end from year to year.

You can use Worksheet 5.1 to compare the per-share information for similar funds.

Management

Good performance reflects good management, so funds with good performance histories are probably managed well. To be sure, look beyond performance and seek the answers to these questions about management:

• *How long has the manager been running the fund? If only for a few years, how has it performed during that period compared with its prior*

WORKSHEET 5.1
PER-SHARE INFORMATION WORKSHEET

	Fund A	Fund B	Fund C
Name of fund			
800 number			
Last year's total return			
Last year's index			
Best year's return 19__			
Best year's index 19__			
Worst year's return 19__			
Worst year's index 19 _			
Last year's expense ratio			
Portfolio turnover rate			
Fund size			
Growing or shrinking assets?			

performance? If performance has improved, the manager has probably brought effective skills to the management table, which will impact future performance. If performance has declined, compare the performance of this fund to that of similar funds, to see if the fault lies with management or with overall market conditions for this type of fund.

• *What other funds does the manager run? How have they performed compared to similar funds?* A good manager should be able to achieve above-average results from most, if not all, the funds he or she manages. If that is not the case, then perhaps favorable recent performance of the fund you are considering is a product more of good fortune than good management.

• *What funds did the manager run before this one, and what was their performance while he or she was at the helm?* Pay particular attention to similar funds; for example, if you are considering investing in a growth fund, and the manager has managed growth funds in the past, that data will probably be more relevant than performance data on a bond fund the manager formerly ran.

• *Is the fund run by one or two individuals, or by a committee?* Experts disagree about whether a committee is superior or inferior to individual management, but at least with a committee you won't have to fear that the fund manager will leave and fund performance will drop. Most funds are managed by one or two people rather than by a group.

In the prospectus, you will usually find information about the manager, other funds that he or she runs, and his or her tenure at this fund. For other answers, call the shareholder services department and ask them for the data you require. If they cannot provide information regarding performance of funds formerly managed by the manager, you may have to call those funds for that information.

Other Sources of Information

If you are new to mutual funds or investments in general, or if you have never read a prospectus before, as you read the prospectus your head may be swimming with terms you don't understand and sentences that seem to have been translated directly from Greek. Don't give up. There's no need to understand every word of what you read the first time, you just need to be aware of what's there. If the prospectus is too daunting, you can gather much of the information that you need from personal finance magazine mutual fund rating charts and from your library's copy of rating service reports by Morningstar or Value Line. Shareholder services may even be able to send you a copy of the rating service reports for the funds you are considering.

If you gather the information you need from personal finance magazine reports, compare it to data contained in the prospectus to be sure that the numbers are approximately the same. The data probably won't match exactly, as the rating periods may not correspond; for example, the prospectus may give information for the year ended December 31, while the magazine figures are updated through June 30.

If you still need more information or you don't understand the information that you have, call the shareholder services representatives and ask them to explain it to you. They are generally well versed on the funds their company sells, and they will be happy to help you get the facts you need to make a sound investment decision.

If you pick a fund that fits your asset mix—a fund that has a reasonably strong past performance history—and you have scanned the prospectus to spot any "red flags," you have done the minimum necessary to invest wisely. Although it is true that past performance doesn't guarantee future results, a fund with strong past performance and continuing good management will probably perform reasonably well in coming years. As author Damon Runyon once wrote, "The race may not be to the swift nor the victory to the strong, but that's how you bet."

6

· · · · · · · ·

STEP 4
Keeping Up with
Your Investments

You've evaluated your investor profile and picked the mutual funds that fit your particular goals, so you may think that there is nothing left to do now but sit back and watch your investment garden grow. Unfortunately you can't ignore your investments, any more than a backyard gardener can relax. Keeping an eye on your investment garden isn't difficult work and won't require a lot of your time, but it *is* important to stay vigilant, weeding and replanting as necessary. And watering your investment garden with regular additions will help your investment crop grow even faster.

Record-Keeping
Each time you invest in a fund you will receive a statement showing the date, the amount invested, the share price, the number of shares purchased, and the total shares you own. Most fund statements also show the current value of the shares you hold.

If you are making regular investments—for example, $100 a month—the statements you receive during the year may be cumulative. For example, the statement you receive in April will reflect, in addition to April's purchase, the details of the purchases you made in January, February, and March. If the statements are cumulative, there is no need to keep the earlier statements. The

April statement will chronicle all your fund activity for the year, so keep that one and throw away any earlier statements for the year.

There are many computer programs you can use to keep track of your investment purchases and reinvested dividends. Some of the better-known programs are Quicken, Andrew Tobias's Managing Your Money, and *Money* magazine's Wealthbuilder, with many more coming on the market. But you don't need a computer to keep up with your money. You can also track your investments by hand, or construct simple worksheets for your computer using a spreadsheet program. Worksheet 6.1 shows a format you can use.

Adding to Your Investments Using Dollar-Cost Averaging

Dollar-cost averaging is a fancy term for investing money over time. In dollar-cost averaging, you invest a set amount each month, acquiring more shares when the price is low and fewer shares when the price is higher. The result is a lower cost per share than if you bought a set number of shares each month.

Dollar-cost averaging isn't easy when you buy individual stocks and bonds, because the commissions are high on small purchases of stocks, and bonds can't be bought in less than $5,000 lots. But mutual funds are heaven-made for dollar-cost averaging, because you can make small regular investments without above-normal costs.

Dollar-cost averaging works better with growth and aggressive growth funds than with income or growth and income funds. That is because growth and aggressive growth funds are more volatile, so they may have wide swings in price from month to month. Therefore you are more likely to find a lower price when you make your monthly investment than you would with a more stable fund.

Dollar-cost averaging has an added advantage, especially with an automatic investment plan, where you invest a set amount each month. It helps keep you from panicking when markets go down. You can be delighted that the market has dropped and you are able to acquire so many more shares that month, rather than become frightened and pull all your money out of a fund just when the

WORKSHEET 6.1
STOCKS OWNED

Date	Share Price	Amount Invested	Dividend Invested	Total Invested	Shares Acquired	Total Shares	Total Value

FUND NAME _____

Totals							

FUND NAME _____

Totals							

FUND NAME _____

Totals							

SUMMARY

Fund name _____

Fund name _____

Fund name _____

Total Portfolio

market reaches bottom. And that is just as it should be. Dollar-cost averaging helps you buy low and hold on, so you can eventually sell high.

Once you realize the market is falling, rejoice! It's time to add even more to your investments. A major downfall of individual investors is that they won't buy when stocks go on sale. When the market is down, they quit investing, or worse yet, pull their money out. When prices zoom up, back in they jump; having missed the chance to buy low, they now enthusiastically buy high.

As a matter of fact, a recent study by Morningstar proved just that. Morningstar compiled the performance results of 219 growth mutual funds for the five years ended May 31, 1994. During that period, the average return of those funds was 12.5 percent. You'd think that the investors would have been pleased, but they weren't. When Morningstar compiled the performance results for actual investors in those funds, they found that, by and large, investors bought each time funds were high and sold in a panic when they declined. As a result, the average return experienced by investors in the funds was a *negative* 2.2 percent!

GETTING RICH $50 AT A TIME

If you add as little as $50 a month to your mutual fund, here's what you can expect.

End of year	6%	8%	10%	12%
1	620	627	634	640
2	1,278	1,305	1,333	1,362
3	1,976	2,040	2,107	2,175
5	3,506	3,698	3,904	4,124
10	8,235	9,208	10,328	11,617
15	14,614	17,417	20,896	25,229
20	23,218	29,647	38,285	49,957
25	34,823	47,868	66,895	94,882
30	50,477	75,014	113,966	176,496
35	71,592	115,459	191,414	324,763
40	100,072	175,714	318,839	594,121

Variations on Dollar-Cost Averaging

With regular dollar-cost averaging, you add the same amount to your fund, month after month. Here are some variations on regular dollar-cost averaging:

Progressive dollar-cost averaging. With progressive dollar-cost averaging, you invest the same amount each month, but you increase the amount of your monthly contribution each year. If you are investing $50 per month now, next year increase your monthly investment to $60, and the year after that to $70. The $10 increase each year will be relatively painless, but it will boost your investments considerably over a number of years.

Value averaging. With value averaging, you decide how much your investments must grow each month. At the end of each month you will compute how much the value of your fund has increased or decreased, and invest enough to bring it to your desired monthly amount. Say you invest $2,000 into a fund initially, and you want your money to grow $200 per month. At the end of the first month, your account is still worth $2,000, so you invest $200 more. You now have $2,200. Next month you want your fund to grow to $2,400, but the market falls and your fund is worth only $2,100. You must invest $300 to bring it up to the $2,400 you desire. (Notice that you are investing more when the shares are cheaper, a hallmark of shrewd investing.) The next month your shares increase in value to $2,700, so you invest nothing, as $2,600 was your goal. If the market stays flat, the next month you'll invest $100 to increase your fund value to $2,800, and so on. You'll be investing less when shares are expensive and more when they are cheaper, and your average cost generally will be less than if you used regular dollar-cost averaging. Try value averaging if you are willing to make monthly computations and have some latitude with the amount you can invest.

Constant-ratio investing. To use constant-ratio investing, first determine what percentage of your overall investment you want each fund to be. Let's say you invest $1,000 into each of two funds, a growth stock fund and a growth and income fund, and you want to invest $200 more each month. At the end of the month, the growth fund has gone up to $1,060, while the growth and income fund is still worth just $1,000. You will allocate $70 of your $200 investment to the growth fund and $130 to the growth and income fund, bringing each fund to $1,130. The next month you will again allocate your investment so the fund values become equal. The computations take considerable effort when several funds are involved, so you may wish to invest a set amount each month into the funds, and add additional amounts each quarter to the funds whose values lag, to shore up the percentages.

Lump-Sum Investing Using Dollar-Cost Averaging
Let's say you just received a hefty bonus, so you want to add $5,000 to your mutual fund investments. If you do so all at once, you run the risk that the market will fall, and you will have invested at just the wrong time. As a matter of fact, with all the ups and downs of the market, no matter when you choose to put the money in, you are likely to see the market dip below that point sometime in the future. On the other hand, if you put $500 into the fund each month for the next ten months, each time the market dips, you'll cheer. That's because you'll be getting more shares of the fund for your money, because the price per share has fallen. You'll be buying low, which gives you a better chance of selling higher in the future. If the market climbs, you'll be buying all the way up, rather than waiting for the "right" time to buy. The shares you acquired earlier in the year will be increasing in value, and your new shares will become more valuable in future months.

INVESTING DURING A BULL MARKET
Dollar-cost averaging for lump sums may not make sense in the early stages of a bull market, or in a bear market that promises quick recovery. When prices are climbing rapidly, you will benefit far more from investing your money early, taking full advantage of the early

growth in value, rather than spreading your investment over several months and losing out on the early price surge. For example, if you invest $1,000 all at once and the price goes up 20 percent, you've made $200. But if you invest only $200 now and defer investing the rest, you'll make only $40 when the fund flourishes.

Rebalancing Your Portfolio

As your mutual fund portfolio grows, you will find that some segments grow faster than others. No fund does well under all market conditions. Sometimes the market favors bonds, and sometimes stocks. Sometimes it favors value investors, and sometimes those who invest for growth. Sometimes large-cap stocks do better than small-cap stocks, and sometimes the opposite is true. In a well-balanced portfolio, when some portions of your holdings are down, others may be doing just fine.

Periodically rebalance your portfolio, bringing it back to its original percentages. You will want to do this at least once a year, and after any large movement up or down in one of the markets. For example, let's say you originally invested $40,000, putting 25 percent of your investment into each of four funds: an aggressive growth fund, a growth fund, an international equity fund, and a bond fund. One year later your investments have grown as follows:

Aggressive growth	$12,700	28% of total
Growth fund	$11,400	25% of total
International equity fund	$11,200	25% of total
Bond fund	$ 9,700	22% of total
Total	$45,000	

To rebalance your fund portfolio, you should sell about $1,500 of the aggressive growth fund, and invest it in the bond fund, so that each fund ends up with 25 percent of the total portfolio value. This strategy may seem strange at first: Why should you sell part of a fund that has done so well, and invest the money in a type of fund that has done less well? It's because throughout economic cycles investments move into and out of the investment spotlight. Funds that have done well in comparison with other types of funds may lag in future years. By rebalancing your portfolio, you'll ride the economic waves. As you sell investments that have *increased* in value and invest the proceeds in funds that have *decreased* in value, you are selling high and buying low, the classic investment strategy. Rebalancing helps you maintain a portfolio that is balanced for risk, and protects your investments in bad times as well as good.

You can use Worksheet 6.2 to compute the amount of each fund you should buy or sell to rebalance your portfolio.

WORKSHEET 6.2

REBALANCING YOUR PORTFOLIO

Type of fund	(A) Current Value	(B) Current Percent	(C) Desired Percent	(D) Desired Value	(A)−(D) Change Needed
Total		100%	100%		

Mutual Funds and Your Tax Return

Investing in mutual funds will complicate your tax life somewhat, as you will have to report dividend income each year, and the gain or loss when you sell shares. Fortunately, most of the reporting is fairly routine. Dividends from the fund will be reported to you on a Form 1099, similar to the form you receive from the bank for interest you have earned on your savings. You will have to pay tax on the dividends even if you asked that they be reinvested in more fund shares. If the dividend income is from municipal bonds, you will report them on your tax return, but will not have to pay tax on them, as they are free from federal tax. If the dividend income is from U.S. Treasury obligations, you will have to pay federal income tax on the dividends, but may receive a break on your state and local income tax returns.

Interest by Any Other Name Is Taxed the Same
All income paid by a mutual fund is called dividend income, even though it would be considered interest income if you owned the underlying bonds or cash funds directly. The 1099 form you receive may also report capital gains distributions to you. This is your share of all gains during the year from selling underlying portfolio assets. Even though you held on to the fund shares and made no sales, you may still have capital gains that must be reported. The capital gains are taxed at your normal federal tax bracket, up to a maximum rate of 28 percent. If your normal federal tax bracket exceeds 28 percent, you will use the special section of Schedule D to compute the tax on capital gains dividends, and the gain or loss on shares you sold that were held longer than a year. Otherwise, simply include the capital gains dividends with your other income in the spaces provided on your tax return.

Mutual funds that invest in foreign securities may send you a Form 1099 that shows you paid foreign taxes on that income. Because you are not required to pay taxes on the same income to two different countries, you will be able to claim credit on your U.S. income tax return for those taxes paid. Use Form 1116 to claim the foreign tax credit.

Reporting Mutual Fund Sales
If you sold shares of your mutual fund during the year, you must report that sale on your tax return. The mutual fund company will send you a 1099-B form detailing the dates you sold shares and the amount you received. Those sales will be reported on Schedule D of your income tax return. If you held the shares for a year or less, you will report the sale as a short-term sale. If you

held the shares for more than a year, you will report the sale as a long-term sale.

Computing the Cost of Shares Sold

When you compute your gain from selling shares in a mutual fund, you are allowed to deduct your original cost of the shares from the sale price. If you purchased all the shares at the same time, your computation will be easy. Simply multiply the shares you have sold by your original cost per share, and that is your cost for tax purposes (called "tax basis").

If you purchased the shares at various times—for example, through dividend reinvestment or dollar-cost averaging—the task of computing your tax basis is a little more difficult. If you have sold *all* your shares of the fund, simply add together all the amounts you invested plus the total of all dividends reinvested, and that is your tax basis.

But what if you sold only part of your fund? Let's say you withdrew $15,000 to purchase a new car. To compute your cost basis using the single-category method, figure the average basis by adding together all the money you've invested, including reinvested dividends, just as above, and then divide it by the number of shares you own. Now multiply the cost per share by the number of shares you have sold. Some mutual fund companies now make the computation automatically and provide you with the average cost of shares you sold.

You can use Worksheet 6.3 to compute your average cost per share.

If you want to use the double-category method, you will make two computations. First compute the average cost of the shares you have owned for more than a year, and then compute the average cost of the shares you have owned for less than a year. You must assume that the shares you sold were the shares you held the longest, unless you have written confirmation from the fund that you asked them to redeem shares acquired more recently.

You may also compute your gain or loss by using the *actual cost* of the shares, instead of the *average cost*. To determine the actual cost,

WORKSHEET 6.3

COMPUTING AVERAGE COST PER SHARE

Year	*(A)* *Total* *Invested*	*(B)* *Dividends* *Reinvested*	*(C)* *Number* *of Shares* *Acquired*
————	————	————	————
————	————	————	————
————	————	————	————
————	————	————	————
————	————	————	————
Total	————	————	————

Add (A) plus (B) ————

Average cost per share (divide by [C]) ————

you will assume that the shares sold were the earliest ones purchased, so look back to your early records to identify the cost of your earliest purchases. Use that cost when you make your computation. For example, assume you invested $2,000 and purchased 200 shares at $10 each, and later invested $1,200 to buy an additional 100 shares at $12. If you now sell 250 shares, your actual cost will be $10 per share for 200 of the shares and $12 per share for the remaining 50 shares. If you like, when you sell shares you can tell the fund in writing which shares are being sold, picking those with the highest cost so as to reduce the taxable gain. For example, you might send the mutual fund company a letter stating, "I would like to redeem the 57 shares I acquired on April 1, 1995." You would then use the actual cost of those shares as your tax basis.

Once you have chosen a method for computing the tax basis for shares sold, you must continue to use that same method for computing the tax basis for additional shares you sell from any fund run by the same family. Most investors take the easy way out, using the average cost per share.

If you sell shares you received as a gift, your tax basis is generally the amount paid by the person who gave you the shares. If you sell the shares at a loss, however, you may have to substitute the value on the date of the gift, if it was lower than the original cost. If you sell shares you inherited, your tax basis is the value of the shares on the date the owner died.

This may all seem complicated at first, but if you keep good records of your investments, or at least don't lose the annual summary statement sent to you by the fund, you'll be able to easily gather the information you need.

7

· · · · · · · ·

STEP 5
Assessing Fund Performance

J ust as recent car buyers continue to peruse car ads for weeks to see how the price they paid compares to current prices, once you invest in mutual funds, you may begin to follow the price of your funds closely, celebrating each day a fund ticks upward and lamenting when it falls.

The financial pages of most newspapers list the highs, lows, and last price each day for most mutual funds. If you subscribe to an on-line service, you can also access fund price through your computer. And most funds maintain an 800 number you can call to find the most recent closing price for the funds.

Don't check the fund prices every day: the change is generally just a few cents one way or the other. Once a week is plenty, and once a month, or even every few months, is adequate. If you dollar-cost average, investing regularly in the fund, you won't have to check at all. The statements you receive from the fund each time you invest will show your purchase price for each transaction this year, and that historic compilation of fund prices will let you see recent price trends.

If one of your funds rises in value while the others remain steady, you may be tempted to add more money to that fund. As the racetrack gamblers say, "Nobody ever bet enough on the winning horse." But just as it would be foolish to bet on the horse that won the last race to win the next one, so might it be foolish to invest in a fund with recent gains, and ignore other funds with solid past performance. Bet on the next race, not the last one. If you chose your funds with care, they probably all have similar chances of turning in good results for the year.

Keeping Abreast

Reading the Financial Pages

The fund tables in your local newspaper have two columns, one headed "NAV," which stands for "net asset value," and the other headed "Buy" or "Offer." The NAV is the price at which you could have sold the fund yesterday. The "buy" column lists the price which you would have had to pay yesterday to buy the fund. The difference between the two prices is the load, or sales charge. If there is no load, the letters "NL" will appear in the buy column. There may be other codes, usually in small letters, that indicate other charges. For example, "r" indicates there is a redemption charge, "p" indicates a 12b-1 fee, and a "t" means the fund is subject to both a redemption charge and a 12b-1 fee. An "x" means the fund just paid a dividend.

On occasion you will see that dashes appear where the prices should be. This doesn't mean that your fund has become worthless, it just indicates that the fund value had not been computed when the table was published that day.

Shareholder Reports

Your mutual funds will send you quarterly or semiannual reports to tell you how the funds are doing. A letter to the shareholders will discuss market conditions and the fund's performance. Most reports also provide a list of the fund's holdings, by industry or sector, so you will know the underlying investments. The shareholder report is generally easy to read. Take a few minutes to read the letter, and glance through the list of holdings for familiar names. You don't need to be concerned about which stocks the fund holds—that's the job of the fund manager—but it may give you some comfort to see that the fund holds stocks of some companies you have actually heard of, and whose products you buy.

Many funds are required to hold annual meetings, so you will receive a proxy card along with an invitation to attend the annual meeting. If you do not plan to attend, sign and return the proxy card, as the company must have a quorum of shareholders present in person or by proxy before the meeting can be held.

Computing Total Return

Remember the old Greyhound bus slogan, "Take the bus, and leave the driving to us"? As a mutual fund investor, let the fund managers worry about the best time to buy or sell—that is what they are paid to do. You can monitor the performance of the manager by comparing the total return for your fund to that of similar funds.

Your mutual fund generates three kinds of income: income distributions, which represent the interest and dividends from the portfolio investments; capital gains distributions, which are the profits the fund makes when it sells securities; and any change in share price since you purchased your shares. The combination of these three factors makes up your total return on your investment.

The Wall Street Journal daily publishes the total return for most funds for various periods of time ranging from four weeks to five years. In addition, most financial magazines publish periodic mutual fund roundups in which they list the total return of the funds.

You may want to compute the total return of your own funds each year. To do so, take the fund value at the end of the year plus any dividends you have received in cash (reinvested dividends are already included in the fund value and so do not need to be added), and divide by the fund value at the beginning of the year. Subtract 1, and what remains is the percentage increase. For example, if your fund was worth $10,000 at the beginning of the year and $12,000 at the end of the year, including reinvested dividends, $12,000 divided by $10,000 is 1.20. Subtract 1, and you'll find that your fund increased .20, or 20 percent.

To compute the total return on your investments, use this simple worksheet:

1. Value at beginning of year   _____
2. Money you added during the year   _____
3. Money you withdrew during the year   _____
4. Net additions / withdrawals (line 2 minus line 3)   _____
5. Divide line 4 by two   _____
6. Average investment (line 1 plus line 5)   _____
7. Value at end of year   _____
8. Total gain (loss) (line 6 minus line 7)   _____
9. Percentage total return (line 8 divided by line 6)   _____%

Deciding When to Sell

To decide whether to keep a mutual fund or to sell your shares and invest in the shares of another, ask yourself this question: If I were analyzing this fund for the first time, and comparing it to other funds with similar investment objectives, is this the fund I would choose? (Use the worksheets on pages 51 and 73 to make this comparison.) If you would choose other funds over the one you now own, then consider selling it.

To evaluate the performance of a fund, you must determine how the fund is doing relative to other funds of its type. If your fund is a small-cap growth fund, how has it performed in relation to other small-cap growth funds? If it is a growth and income fund, measure it by that yardstick. If all funds of that type are doing poorly in today's economy, you'll just have to wait out the storm, unless you switch to a different type of fund.

Here's how to make your comparison: First, evaluate the performance for the past three years in comparison to a standard index (see Table 5.1 on page 66). If the fund has done well in any of those three years, it is probably too early to decide to sell. Even the best-run fund falls on hard times, but will work its way out if given time. If your fund has not performed well for any of the three years, compare its performance to that of similar funds in which you might invest. If these funds have done better in all three years, it is probably time to switch.

Don't add new funds to your portfolio every time you have money to invest. Keep your number of funds constant, and weed out the weak performers. There should be a purpose for each fund you hold, and holding two funds that are alike is a no-no: Get rid of the weaker of the two, and place the money with the better fund. This does not mean you can't have two funds of the same type. For example, you can hold two international equity funds; if one focuses on European stocks and the other pursues emerging world markets, they are not alike. Similarly, two growth stock funds will be dissimilar if one concentrates on value investing while the other leans toward traditional growth stocks.

Mutual Fund Investment Mistakes

Here are some of the most common mistakes made by beginning mutual fund investors:

Driving exclusively with a rear-view mirror. Although past performance is important, consider all factors that will predict future returns. The most important factor of all is fund objective.

Looking at averages rather than annual returns. A fund may have a great five- or ten-year average if it had a spectacular year or two several years ago, but it may have experienced mediocre performance ever since. Conversely, a fund that has recently come under new management may have great recent returns after a dismal past, and so the five- or ten-year averages won't be reasonable indicators of possible future performance.

Ignoring cycles. Stay aware that different investing approaches, such as value or growth, tend to flourish in cycles. For example, if value-oriented funds have done well during the past three years, consider growth-oriented funds for your future investments.

Jumping ship too quickly. Even the best-managed fund can steer into choppy waters, and it will take time for it to steer clear and regain its balance again. The more volatile the fund, the more frequently it will encounter a choppy patch. Give your fund a year to eighteen months to bounce back after it begins underperforming its peers. If it hasn't weathered the storm within two years, then it's probably time to bail out.

Failing to rebalance. It's tough to sell shares in a winner and invest in funds that haven't performed as well recently, but that's just what you should do regularly to take advantage of changing economic cycles. For example, if the stock portion of your portfolio has done well in relation to bonds, either sell a part of your stock funds and reinvest in bond funds, or channel future investments into bond funds until your portfolio is rebalanced to its original percentages.

Acquiring funds without a plan. Some amateur investors, even those who have been investing for some time, acquire funds because they've done well in the past, without regard for whether they fit into their overall plan. Such an investor's portfolio may end up with several funds that are similar, and without some types of fund that are crucial to portfolio performance. You probably need no more than five to eight different funds in your mutual fund portfolio: before you buy a new one, decide which fund you are going to sell. If you can't bear to part with a fund because it performs so well, you probably don't need the new fund.

Trying to time the market. In market timing, your goal is to invest just as the market begins to climb, and to unload your investments just before the market declines. Unfortunately, just like developing that perfectly timed golf swing, market timing is easy in theory and hard in practice. Professional market timers often miss the mark, and novices haven't got a chance. By the time you realize the market is falling and you begin to sell, you'll likely have experienced a considerable drop in value already. And once you become courageous enough to get back in, the market will probably have experienced many of its best trading days. By attempting to time the market, you experience some of the losses and miss much of the profits. That is why most market timers don't do as well as buy-and-hold investors.

Rearranging funds too often. Don't expect each of your funds to outperform all the others, year after year. Some of your funds will perform better than others this year, but next year your star performer may take a backseat to a new star in your firmament of funds. Bill Cosby once said that he didn't know the key to success, but he knew the key to failure was trying to please everybody. In mutual funds, the key to failure is constantly rearranging your investments, trying to capture every high performer. It's impossible to do. Like a child chasing fireflies, you can't capture all the brightest ones. A portfolio of bright performers that are all above average, like the children in Garrison Keillor's Lake Wobegon, should be your goal. That goal is well within your reach.

PART II

GROWING YOUR
MUTUAL FUND
PORTFOLIO

8

• • • • • • • •

HOW ECONOMIC CONDITIONS AFFECT YOUR MUTUAL FUNDS

I t is easy to buy and sell mutual funds. This is both a blessing and a curse. Mutual funds *should* be a long-term investment, but the ease with which money can be moved from fund to fund with just a telephone call encourages folks to try to time the market, which is very difficult to do.

Market Timing

The future is difficult to predict, because it keeps turning into today. All we know for sure is that everything is in a state of flux, subject to change. And that is both the delight and the downfall of market timers.

If you could time the market just right, you would invest just as the market begins to move upward and sell your mutual funds just before the market drops. Unfortunately, there is no one to tell you when the market hits bottom or to shout "Everyone out of the water!" when the market wave crests, so you can recognize those extremes only in retrospect. The advice to buy at the bottom and sell at the top is about as helpful as these directions given by one bus rider to another: "Watch me, and get off the bus one stop before I do." You'll have to travel farther along the route before you can discern the place at which you should have gotten off.

Market timers don't profess to be able to guess the exact peak, or predict the exact bottom. What most market timers try to do is take advantage of most of a market's rally, investing just after the market begins its rise, while avoiding most of its decline by selling as prices begin to drop. Unfortunately, their timing strategies often lead them out of the market just before an unexpected rally, or leave them fully invested during a sudden decline. Charles Ellis, a renowned investment guru, wrote in his book *Investment Policy*, "The evidence on investment managers' success with market timing is impressive—and overwhelmingly negative."

Market timing can be very costly taxwise, because each time you trade at a profit, you incur a tax liability. The buy-and-hold investor pays far less tax, as he or she pays tax only on the actual trades made by the mutual fund. Any increase in the value of fund shares isn't taxed until the shares are finally sold.

When to Buy, When to Sell
The market waxes and wanes each trading day, and in any given week there will probably be days in which the market rose and days in which it declined. Market timers are looking for larger swings in the market than just daily ups and downs. They are concerned with the general momentum of the market over a period of months, or even years. And that sort of movement is far easier to see at a distance, in your rear-view mirror.

In general, you should buy stocks about six months before economic recovery begins, and sell about six months before the start of a recession. It sounds easy enough to do in retrospect, but it's darn difficult to predict. If you want to time the market, your first investment should be a crystal ball.

To add to the confusion, the experts often disagree when markets shift direction. For example, if the economy heats up and the market suddenly heads south after a period of rapid growth, some will say a bear market has begun, while others detect only a short-lived "market correction" and predict the market will shortly continue its bullish trend. Who is right? Only time will tell. If the "correction" is prolonged, the experts will finally all agree that a bear market has begun. If the market recovers quickly and continues upward, it might appear that the recent drop was indeed just a correction—but true bear-market pessimists might say that the new upward movement is just a short-lived rally. Either way, if you got out at the wrong time, or stayed in when you should have gotten out, you will have mistimed the market, and your investment return will suffer.

Bears Die Quickly

A bear market is generally defined by a stock market decline of 20 percent or more. Less than that is called a correction. A bear market can be a buying opportunity, but don't wait too long, because bear markets tend to be over quickly. After the worst bear market in modern history, in 1973–1974, it took three and a half years for the stock market to get back to even. But in milder bear markets, recovery happens in less than two years. There have been fourteen bear markets since 1926, and on average they have lasted sixteen months before they bottomed out and started an upward trek.

Of course, if you could predict the peaks and valleys, it would be profitable to avoid bear markets altogether. But even if you had stayed fully invested through bear market after bear market, since 1926 you would have made 10.3 percent annually on your money, even though the market declined in one-quarter of those years. The odds were only 11 percent that you would lose money if you invested for any five-year period, and only 4 percent that you would lose money during any ten-year period. You never would have lost money if you invested for twenty years or longer.

Bonds are safer, from the standpoint of volatility. If you invested in bonds, you would never have lost money over any five-year period during those years. But there is a price to be paid for that relative stability: the average return on bonds since 1926 was only 5.3 percent, half the average return on stocks.

Market timers rely on certain economic indicators to tell them when to buy and when to sell. Each market timer relies on a different set of predictive formulas, but they all share one thing: fallibility. The *Hulbert Financial Digest*, a newsletter that tracks investment newsletters, followed fifteen market-timing newsletters for the ten years ended December 31, 1992. In that period, only two of the newsletters outperformed the S&P 500, one by less than 1 percent and the other by little more than 2 percent. The worst of the market timers underperformed the market by 6 percent! Studies have shown that a market timer has to be right more than 70 percent of the time to beat the buy-and-hold investor, and few market timers can perform that accurately.

Market Timing Causes Tax Problems

Each time a market timer sells a fund and buys a new one, he or she triggers a trade that must be reported on the tax return. If the trade results in a gain, there are taxes to be paid, and that can eat up any profits from market timing in a hurry, unless the investment is part of a retirement plan, in which case no taxes will be due until you withdraw money from the plan. Be sure to consider the tax consequences along with the other risks before you attempt to time the market.

Market Timing Barely Outperforms the Long-Term Investor

The investment firm Piper Jaffray studied what would have happened if you had invested $1,000 a year in Standard & Poor's 500 stock index every year from 1960 to 1993. If you had bought at the market bottom each year, the best time to invest, you would have made 10.6 percent a year. But if you weren't so lucky, and bought at exactly the wrong time, as the market peaked each year, you would still have earned 10.4 percent. So there you have it—market timing isn't the answer. Investing early, staying invested, and adding to your investments regularly are the key to success.

History shows us that bull markets outlast bear markets. Stocks rise, on average, during 70 percent of the years, falling only three years out of ten. That is why a long-term investor can do well even without trying to time the market. Buy in, and stay in, and let the rising tide carry your boat higher over the long term.

IS THE BULL MARKET ENDING?

Here are some of the clues that a bull market is coming to an end:
- Interest rates rise for three-month Treasury bills.
- The Federal Reserve, which meets several times each year, raises the discount rate for banks three consecutive times in an attempt to stave off inflation.
- The Department of Commerce's index of leading economic indicators is down three months in a row, signaling an impending recession.
- The stock market indexes are moving up, but the advance/decline line (the difference between the gainers and losers each day) is dropping.
- One stock market index is moving up, but others are declining.
- The dividend yield on the S&P 500 is below 3 percent, and the price/earnings ratio is above 20.

Economic Cycles

If you want to try market timing, you can subscribe to market-timing newsletters, or watch the economic news yourself. Here is how economic cycles affect stock market prices.

You can think of economic cycles in four stages. First, as recession ends and a growth stage begins, people begin to buy because interest rates are declining and inflation has slowed. In the second stage, the economy continues to expand, as more people accept that recession is over, and businesses increase production and hire more people. In the third stage of recovery, increased borrowing to finance production and consumer purchases takes its toll, and interest rates and inflation both rise. And finally, recession begins as the federal reserve raises interest rates, consumers slow their buying, and production slows.

Economic growth cycles are much longer than periods of recession. For example, in the 1960s we had 106 months of growth followed by 11 months of recession. In the 1970s a 36-month growth period was followed by 16 months of recession; then a 58-month growth cycle preceded 6 months of recession. In the early 1980s, after an atypical brief seesaw of 12 months of growth followed by 16 months of recession, we enjoyed a long growth period interrupted by a short recession in the early 1990s.

When investors anticipate growth, the stock market turns bullish. When recession is in the wind, the bears take over. For that reason, the stock market is a very accurate leading indicator of economic cycles. The stock market turns bearish and begins to decline about six months before we enter recession, and takes an upswing about six months before economic recovery begins.

Even though the beginnings of recessions and recoveries are well documented historically, they are hard to pinpoint at the time. Unless you have a crystal ball and can predict a future economic change, it is difficult to invest or disinvest six months before that change happens. Furthermore, we aren't positive that we are in recession or recovery until about six months after it begins, because it takes the National Bureau of Economic Research at least that long to date a business-cycle turn.

Economic Crisis

Do you fear the stock market will crash and lose half its value overnight? The experts say that isn't likely. Stock market speculation and program trading have been severely collared by federal regulations since the stock market crash of 1987, and now complex trading brakes kick in to cushion the fall when the stock market begins to slide. An economic crisis now would probably creep up rather than crash, giving you plenty of time to redistribute your investments. Remember that even in 1987, before the new regulations were in effect, stocks lost far less than half their value, and recovered quickly.

A creeping economic crisis would likely come in the guise of inflation or deflation. In times of rampant inflation or deflation, it is best to keep your money in U.S. government short-term bond funds or money market funds, because they are more stable than long-term bonds. A gold fund might be a good hedge against inflation or deflation as well, as the price of gold tends to increase in times of inflation or economic crisis.

Once the economy signals the crisis is ending, funnel your money back into the stock and bond markets as soon as possible. Economic recovery can be quite rapid, and much of the market movement may be in the early months of the rally. If you miss the beginning days of a rally, you will lose out on much of the market gains.

Other indicators to keep in mind are price/earnings (P/E) ratios and dividend yields. The market is considered expensive when price/earnings ratios approach 20, and cheap when P/E ratios fall below 10. That range gives you an idea of the best time to sell or buy. When dividend yields drop below 3 percent, the stock market has become expensive. When they are 6 percent or more, the market is cheap and it is probably time to buy.

DON'T BE LATE FOR THE PARTY

The major problem with market timing is that much of the total gain from a bull market tends to occur rapidly at the beginning of a market recovery. That's why it is more important to be in the bull markets from the beginning than it is to avoid the bear markets. So if a market timer, to make sure the market upswing is genuine, sits on the sidelines as a bull market begins, he is apt to miss a great deal of the profits. Unfortunately, most market timers concentrate on avoiding bear market declines rather than on capturing all of a bull market's profits. That is why few market timers beat the buy-and-hold investor.

Choosing the Right
Baskets for Your Nest Eggs

Asset allocation comes in many different forms. The most risky way of allocating your assets is market timing—when you perceive that economic change is imminent, you take your eggs out of the stock basket and put them into another basket. To paraphrase Mark Twain's Pudd'nhead Wilson: When you put all your eggs in one basket, you have to watch that basket very carefully.

At the other end of the asset allocation scale is strategic allocation: you allocate your assets among stocks, bonds, and cash in accordance with your ability to withstand risk and with how long it will be before you need the money.

In the middle is a strategy called "tactical asset allocation" (TAA). Using computers to predict which categories—stocks, bonds, or cash—will perform the best in the near future, TAA managers frequently move assets back and forth among the categories. And often the TAA managers, through these gyrations, beat the market by a wide margin.

Can you get in on this game? Perhaps you already have: your employer's pension funds may use tactical asset allocation. If you own an asset allocation fund directly or through your 401(k) plan, that fund may practice this strategy.

Unfortunately, asset allocation funds did not perform quite as well in the past five years as did balanced funds, which invest in a set mix of stocks and bonds in constant proportions. As they shift investments from one category to another, the tactical asset allocation funds can also incur more trading costs and capital gains tax than more sedate balanced funds, and these additional costs reduce the profits of asset allocation funds.

Well-timed buying and selling in a well-managed asset allocation fund will probably improve your portfolio's performance. But if you invest in a fund that uses tactical asset allocation, do so with only part of your money. Remember, this is a market-timing approach, and you don't want to jeopardize your entire investment portfolio if the timing is wrong.

Keep your expectations reasonable. Benjamin Graham, renowned for his book on asset allocation, *The Intelligent Investor,* once wrote, "To achieve *satisfactory* results is easier than most people realize; to achieve *superior* results is harder than it looks." Unfortunately, in chasing superior results, many people, especially those who attempt to time the market, fail to achieve even satisfactorily.

Achieving satisfactory results also takes less time than most people realize. To buy and hold takes little time, but if you want to be a more active investor, practice buy-and-hold tactics with three-quarters of your portfolio, and do all the juggling you want with the other one-quarter. That way you can experiment with funds that use different strategies, or chase the hot funds, while still sticking to your basic allocation scheme.

Other Investing Techniques

Value Investing

Value investing is similar to bargain-hunting in the department stores. Just as you look through the racks seeking top quality for a discounted price, the value investor emphasizes low price/ earnings and price-to-book ratios, looking for an out-of-favor company that is trading for less than the total value of its net assets, or one whose earnings represent a great return on its current price. Value investors are defensive when compared to growth investors, who look for companies that will grow faster than the competition. Because of its more conservative approach, value investing works best in times of economic contraction and in the early stages of bull markets. In the later stages of a bull market, when the economy is booming, growth stocks generally outperform value. But for the long-term investor, either style works well. Over the ten years from 1984 to 1994, value stocks returned 15.4 percent a year and growth stocks grew 14.4 percent.

Socially Responsible Investing

Over the past ten years, a number of socially responsible mutual funds have sprung up, and many of them are doing quite well.

These funds have both negative social screens, which identify the bad traits of companies in which they won't invest, and positive social screens, which recognize the good traits of the companies in which they choose to place investment dollars.

Negative screens weed out EPA violators and polluters; companies that deal in nuclear power, weapons production, alcohol, gambling, and tobacco; and human rights violators.

These funds seek out companies with good records for environmental protection, advancement of women and minorities, occupational health and safety, strong employee and customer relations, and product quality and safety. There are even municipal bond funds for investors who prefer to buy bonds that fund education, housing, or environmental protection and cleanup.

Critics of social investing have argued that by limiting your investments to socially responsible companies, you are limiting your ability to make shrewd investment decisions. Some mutual fund companies that have been practicing socially responsible investing for many years, such as the Calvert Group, have racked up impressive investment returns. The long-term investment results of social investing pioneers show how wrong the critics are.

As with any investment, the most moderate approach is to invest with pros who have been managing funds for at least five years. Today there is more than $625 billion in investments that are socially screened, and new funds are being formed regularly. Though some of the newer funds may prove to be excellent, give them some time to build a positive track record before you jump in.

In social investing, you should remember your investment goals in choosing your investments. If you need funds for use in the near future, an ethically managed money market fund is best. If you want long-term growth, a number of socially responsible growth funds is available. To balance your income between current income and growth, a balanced fund that follows the principles of social investing would be best. And as with all investing, putting money into the fund on a regular basis through dollar-cost averaging will yield better investment results than investing a lump sum.

9

. . . .

INVESTING FOR RETIREMENT

Whether you are twenty-something, sixty-something, or something in between, it's time to check your retirement plan (or create one) to be sure you'll have enough income when it's time to retire. For today's retiree, Social Security provides about 20 percent of living expenses, less than one week's income a month. Pensions provide only 15 percent of the income retirees need. How do retirees fund the other 65 percent of their expenses? About 25 percent comes from part-time jobs, and the rest from savings. Don't put off saving for retirement, even if you are young—remember, it wasn't raining when Noah built the ark.

The sooner you get started, the better off you'll be. As a matter of fact, if you began investing a set amount each month into mutual funds when you were eighteen and stopped when you were twenty-six, letting the money continue to grow but never adding more money, at age sixty-five you'd have as much money as someone who didn't start investing until age thirty-five and kept investing each month until age sixty-five. The earlier you start, the more your money will grow. Here's a table that shows how much you'll have to save each month to amass a retirement nest egg.

TABLE 9.1

MONTHLY SAVINGS NEEDED TO REACH YOUR RETIREMENT GOAL

		Monthly Savings Needed to Amass			
Your age	*Years to Retirement*	*$250,000*	*$500,000*	*$750,000*	*$1,000,000*
25	40	95	190	286	380
30	35	139	278	416	555
35	30	205	410	615	820
40	25	309	617	926	1,234
45	20	480	960	1,440	1,920
50	15	789	1,577	2,366	3,154
55	10	1,444	2,889	4,333	5,777
60	5	3,492	6,984	10,475	13,968

Let's say you are forty years old, and you want to retire on $50,000 a year in today's dollars. In twenty-five years, assuming 4 percent inflation, it will take $135,000 a year to pay for your living expenses. If Social Security provides $35,000 a year, and your employer's retirement plan plus part-time work provides $60,000, you'll still need $40,000 a year to live. That means you'll need a nest egg of about $500,000. Look at Table 9.1. If you start now to build a $500,000 nest egg, you must save and invest $617 each month. Don't you wish you'd started saving when you were twenty-five, so you would have had to save only $190 each month? You can't turn back the clock, so you'd better start saving now before things get worse.

If you can't save $617 a month, begin saving something. You can save less now and increase your monthly savings each year. For example, save $250 a month this year, $300 next year, and $350 the year after that. To increase your long-term investment return, be sure to stash your retirement money in a portfolio designed for a Striver's goals.

To compute how much you need to save each month to meet your own retirement goals, fill out Worksheet 9.1.

WORKSHEET 9.1

YOUR RETIREMENT NEEDS

1. Annual income needs in retirement (today's $$)   _____
2. Less annual Social Security benefits   _____
3. Less annual pension benefits (today's $$)   _____
4. Less income you'll earn in retirement   _____
5. Retirement income needed at 65, in
   today's dollars (line 1 minus lines 2–4)   _____
6. Amount needed by retirement, in today's
   dollars (line 5 multiplied by 22)   _____
7. Amount already saved for retirement,
   including IRAs   _____
8. Value of savings at retirement, in today's dollars
   (line 7 times Investment Growth Factor below)   _____
9. Savings still needed, in today's dollars
   (line 6 minus line 8)   _____
10. Annual amount you must save (line 9 times
    Annual Savings Factor below)   _____

Years until retirement	Investment Growth Factor	Annual Savings Factor
5	1.16	0.188
10	1.34	0.087
15	1.56	0.054
20	1.81	0.037
25	2.09	0.027
30	2.43	0.021

To squeeze more money out of your budget, reduce your current tax crunch by sheltering as much as you can in tax-deferred retirement plans. Money you invest in retirement plans is tax-deductible, reducing your current tax bite, so you can afford to invest even more. Also consider investing in nondeductible IRAs and variable annuities so you can delay paying taxes on your investment earnings as long as possible. Although the money you invest isn't tax-deductible, the income these investments earn isn't taxed to you until you withdraw it.

Retirement Plans

Retirement plans are your best form of tax-sheltered investment. With retirement plans, not only are your earnings protected from current taxation, but the amount you invest is deductible. It's as though your generous Uncle Sam said, "I'll tell you what, my friend, I'll match every $2 you put away with an interest-free loan of $1, and you won't have to repay me until you retire." With an interest-free loan from Uncle Sam, everything that Sam's money earns belongs to you, less the taxes you'll eventually pay on those earnings. If you invest the money for several years, that can amount to a tidy sum.

Don't Shelter Your Retirement Plan

If you are investing in a retirement plan, you don't need to worry about paying tax on the interest and dividends, or on capital gains when you sell plan investments. You won't pay tax until you ultimately withdraw the money, and meanwhile, your investments will be growing tax-deferred. Because retirement plans are already tax-deferred, it doesn't make sense to put tax-free investments, such as municipal bonds, or tax-deferred investments, such as deferred annuities, into a retirement plan.

The same is true of growth funds. Most growth funds provide some tax deferral because they pay only small dividends, which must be included on your tax return. The increase in value of the growth fund portfolio is taxable to you only when the fund sells the underlying stock it holds, or when you sell your shares of the fund.

If your investment mix calls for investments in bonds, equity income funds, and growth funds, put the bond and equity income portions of your portfolio into your retirement plan, because there the dividends are sheltered from current taxation. The growth fund, which is already partly sheltered from income taxes, would be best held outside the retirement plan. If you invest retirement plan money *and* nonretirement money in growth funds, first select the funds in which you wish to invest, then find the portfolio turnover rate for each fund in the prospectus. Invest the retirement plan money in the fund with the highest portfolio turnover rate. That fund will produce the greatest amount of capital gains income each year, and your retirement plan will shelter that income from current taxation.

Choose the Best Retirement Plans for You

The Internal Revenue Code has given its tax-deferral blessing to many different types of retirement plans. Unfortunately, the rules governing the plans for which you are eligible and how much you can invest are sometimes daunting. Here are some of the retirement plans that are available and a brief synopsis of the rules regarding each one.

IRAs

An IRA is an excellent way to sock away money you won't need until retirement. You may invest up to $2,000 per year in an IRA, which can be put into a variety of investments, such as certificates of deposit, stocks, bonds, annuities, and mutual funds. About 25 percent of all money invested in IRAs is invested in mutual funds.

You can make deductible IRA contributions if you have earned income or alimony, and you and your spouse are not covered by a company retirement plan. If your company's retirement plan is a profit-sharing plan and your employer makes no contribution to the plan this year, your IRA contribution will be deductible as if your employer had no plan.

If your income is less than $25,000 ($40,000 if you are married), your contribution will be tax-deductible even if you are covered under a company plan. Your contribution will be partially tax-deductible if you earn between $25,000 and $35,000 ($40,000 and $50,000 if married).

For example, let's say you are single and earn $30,000. If you are not covered under an employer's retirement plan, you can contribute to an IRA and deduct up to $2,000 each year. However, if your employer covers you under a retirement plan, your tax-deductible contribution to an IRA is limited to $1,000. If you earn over

$35,000, you can't deduct any contributions if you are covered by a retirement plan at work.

A contribution of $2,000 a year may not seem like much, but it can grow over the years. Here is a chart that shows how much $2,000, invested year after year, will become.

Number of years	6%	8%	10%	12%
5	12,000	12,700	13,400	14,200
10	27,900	31,300	35,100	39,300
15	49,300	58,600	69,900	83,500
20	78,000	98,800	126,000	161,400
25	116,300	157,900	216,400	298,700
30	167,600	244,700	361,900	540,600
35	236,200	372,200	596,300	966,900
40	328,100	559,600	973,700	1,718,300

(RATE OF RETURN)

All mutual funds except tax-exempt funds make good IRA investments. If your money will be in an IRA for at least ten years, use the Striver portfolio to allocate your IRA investments. If the money will be there for twenty years or longer, and you are a Daredevil, you may wish to invest exclusively in growth, maximum growth, and international equity funds.

IRA TRANSFERS

IRA transfers are easy to make. Transferring your IRA funds into a different mutual fund within the same family of funds usually requires no more than a phone call. If you want to transfer your money to a new family of funds, just request a form from the new mutual fund. On that form you give your account number with the old mutual fund and ask for a transfer to the new fund. The new fund will take care of the rest.

Most mutual funds charge you a custodial fee, generally $10 per fund per year. Some cap the total IRA custodial fees at $30 or so a year for funds within their family, and some, such as Fidelity, waive the fee if your total IRA investments are above a certain amount, generally $5,000.

Most funds give you a choice of writing a check for the IRA fee, or having it deducted from your IRA contribution. If you pay by check, the IRA fee counts as a miscellaneous itemized deduction on your tax return. If you claim the standard deduction instead of itemizing, or don't exceed the 2-percent-of-income floor for miscellaneous itemized deductions, you will receive no deduction for the fee if you pay it by check. Instead of writing a check, have the fee deducted from your IRA. Over the years the fees mount up, and by deducting the fees from the IRA you may save $100 or so in taxes. It's not a lot, but why throw $100 away?

GETTING THE MOST FROM YOUR IRA

If you have been contributing to Individual Retirement Accounts over the years, or have rolled a lump-sum pension distribution into an IRA, you have taken solid steps toward building a strong retirement nest egg. Analyze your IRA investments to make sure that they fit the appropriate portfolio for you (Conserver, Builder, or Striver) and your risk profile (Defensive, Easygoing, or Daredevil). Also review your IRA accounts to be sure you aren't making some of the following blunders. These common blunders can keep you from getting the greatest income possible when you retire.

Blunder #1. Too many IRA accounts. If you have been investing in IRAs since they were created in 1976, you may have as many as eighteen different IRA accounts scattered among banks, stockbrokers, and mutual funds, and you are paying annual fees for each account. You can save hundreds of dollars each year in account fees by consolidating your accounts into a few mutual funds. Some mutual fund companies eliminate annual fees if you have multiple funds within the same family, or if your investments add up to $5,000 or more.

Blunder #2. The wrong investments. Don't invest all your IRA money in low-interest short-term cash investments such as certificates of deposit or money market accounts. Even a Defensive Conserver who will be withdrawing her money in three years or less should take a little more risk than that to create greater returns. If your money will remain in the IRA for longer than three years, you are a Builder or a Striver, and you'll get a greater long-term return by investing in some solid stock mutual funds on a regular basis. Increasing your average annual investment yield just 2 percent will result in 50 percent more return over twenty years.

Blunder #3. Sheltering your tax shelter. Your IRA is sheltered from tax until you withdraw from it. Municipal bond income is sheltered from tax forever. Although you can invest your IRA money in any type of mutual fund you care to, don't combine these two tax shelters by investing IRA money in a municipal bond fund. Municipal bonds yield less income than is available elsewhere, and if a municipal bond fund is part of your IRA, the income will be fully taxable when you retire and withdraw the money.

Blunder #4. Investing too late. Most people like to delay tax payments until the last minute, so that they can earn as much interest as possible on the money before they send it to Uncle Sam. Your strategy with IRA investments should be different. Although you have until April 15 to contribute to your IRA, you should make IRA contributions as early as possible. IRA contributions made early in the year will earn on a tax-deferred basis all year. It may not sound as if it would make much difference, but you'd be surprised. Making your $2,000 annual contributions at the beginning of each year rather than fifteen months later will result in thousands of extra dollars at retirement. On the next page is a table that shows the difference, for an IRA that earns an average of 10 percent per year.

As you can see, if you consistently invest $2,000 on January 1 of each year rather than waiting until April 15 of the next year, over a forty-year period you will amass an extra $129,700 (the difference between $973,700 and $844,000). Even after only five years of

End of year	Contributions 1/1	Contributions 4/15
5	$ 13,400	$ 9,800
10	35,100	28,500
15	69,900	58,900
20	126,000	107,600
25	216,400	186,000
30	361,900	312,500
35	596,300	516,100
40	973,700	844,000

investing on January 1 instead of April 15, you'll have an extra $3,600 ($13,400, as compared to $9,800).

Simplified Employee Pension Plan (SEP–IRA)

An SEP–IRA (Simplified Employee Pension Plan) is similar to an IRA. It is available only to those who are self-employed or have commission-based income, such as real estate agents. If you pass muster, you may contribute as much as 15 percent of your annual net business income, to a maximum of $30,000, to an IRA under an SEP plan. If you have employees, you must contribute to IRAs for their benefit as well. As with an IRA, you have until April 15 of the following year to make your contribution for the prior year, and if you file for an extension to file your income tax return, you can extend the time for making your contribution as well, all the way to October 15.

You can contribute to an SEP–IRA even if you are covered under an employer's retirement plan. For example, assume you are employed as a salaried advertising copywriter and contribute to the 401(k) plan your employer provides. If you are a freelance writer on the side, you may also contribute up to 15 percent of your net income from freelancing to an SEP–IRA.

Defined-Contribution Keogh Plans

A defined-contribution Keogh plan allows self-employed people to put as much as 25 percent of their income away for retirement, up to a maximum of $30,000 per year. The Keogh plan must cover all qualified employees, and must be established by December 31 of the first year you intend to make contributions to the plan, although the actual contributions don't have to be made until the following April 15. The Keogh also has more extensive setup and filing requirements than the IRA or SEP, and often requires reports to the IRS every year to three years. Thus, many self-employed people with no employees find that the SEP–IRA is less cumbersome than the Keogh to establish and maintain.

If you have employees and experience frequent employee turnover, a Keogh plan will provide you more flexibility than an SEP–IRA. With a Keogh plan, you have the ability to adjust vesting within certain limits, so that employees who work for a short period of time receive only limited retirement benefits.

Defined-Benefit Keogh Plans

If you want to sock away more into a Keogh plan than is allowed in a defined-contribution Keogh plan or an SEP–IRA, a defined-benefit Keogh is the ticket. In this type of plan, you provide for set benefits at retirement, for example, 60 percent of the average of your final three years' compensation. The amount that you can contribute to the plan is then calculated actuarially, and often greatly exceeds the amount you could otherwise contribute. Defined-benefit Keoghs are more cumbersome than defined-contribution plans, as they require the services of an actuary each year in addition to the other paperwork requirements of a Keogh.

401(k) Plans

These salary-reduction plans must be set up by an employer for the benefit of the company employees. If you are employed by a company that offers a 401(k) plan (called a 403[b] or TSA if you work for an educational institution, hospital, or public charity), you can contribute a certain percentage of your salary, specified by your employer's plan (generally between 5 and 25 percent of your salary), up to a maximum of $9,240 for 1995 ($9,500 for a TSA), and your contribution will be deducted from the taxable wages that appear on your W-2 form. Many employers also match the amount that you contribute to a 401(k) plan, to encourage employee savings through the plan. You won't pay tax on 401(k) contributions, employer matching amounts, or plan earnings until you withdraw the money at retirement.

As with other retirement plans, including IRAs, the object is to amass as much as you can by investing in the plan for as long a period of time as possible. Here are some of the mistakes that 401(k) participants make:

• *Not investing enough.* Although plans generally allow you to contribute 10 percent or more to a 401(k) plan, up to $9,500 or so a year, many employees contribute far less. As a matter of fact, the average eligible employee contributes only 5 percent or so of his or her salary into a 401(k) plan.

• *Not taking advantage of employer matching.* If your employer matches your contributions 100 percent, that means with every dollar you contribute you immediately double your money. You won't find better odds than that, even in Las Vegas or Atlantic City, because it's a sure thing: put in your dollar, and it instantly doubles. It's an offer you shouldn't refuse.

• *Not investing your tax savings.* For every three dollars you invest, the government reduces the taxes withheld from your paycheck by about one dollar. That means you can afford to contribute four dollars, not three. Do it! You'll end up with 33 percent more retirement income when you begin drawing benefits.

• *Not investing for the long term.* Your 401(k) money will be in the plan for a long time, so don't stash it in guaranteed income or short-term bonds. If your 401(k) plan offers growth or maximum appreciation funds, that is where the bulk of your money should be if you are a Builder or a Striver.

• *Not taking advantage of plan borrowing.* Many 401(k) plans allow you to borrow from your plan and pay the money back at current interest rates over five years. That means that you can contribute the money you are saving for your children's education to the 401(k) plan, take advantage of employer matching and tax deferral, and then borrow it out again to pay for the children's education.

• *Not rolling over plan distributions when you leave your job.* Many employees take the money and run when they leave employment. Roll the money over into your IRA rather than spending it, or you will be back to ground zero in your retirement planning. If you want to roll the money into your next employer's plan, be sure to roll the 401(k) distribution from your current plan into a new rollover IRA you set up exclusively for that purpose. Don't commingle the money with other IRA funds, or you won't be able to roll it over to your new employer's plan.

Retirement Plan Distributions

If you receive a lump-sum distribution from a retirement plan, it is best to roll it over into an IRA so you won't pay taxes on it all at once. Tucked away in your IRA, it can grow tax-deferred until you need it and draw it out, bit by bit. If you don't roll it over into an IRA, you may also be eligible for five- or ten-year forward averaging if you meet certain age requirements. Five- or ten-year forward averaging allows you to compute tax on the money as though you had received it over a five- or ten-year period, which will generally reduce the rate at which the money is taxed and thus reduce the taxes you have to pay on the distributions. But unless you absolutely need the money now, you'll be better off depositing it into the IRA and forgoing the advantages of forward averaging.

To roll over the plan distributions to your IRA, open up an IRA account with the IRA custodian who will be handling all or part of the money. For example, if you've decided to invest in the T. Rowe Price family of funds, you will open an IRA with T. Rowe Price and ask the retirement plan to send your money there. With the money sent directly to the IRA custodian, you will avoid the 20 percent withholding tax that would be imposed if the money were sent directly to you.

Now you have two choices: to invest your money all at once, or to dollar-cost average. To invest all your money now, simply ask the mutual fund company to apportion the money among the funds you have chosen. For example, if you want to invest 50 percent of the plan distributions in growth funds and 25 percent each in a bond fund and an equity income fund, pick the funds within the mutual fund family and ask that the money be apportioned in these percentages. If you don't want to invest all your money in the same family of funds, you will need to open up IRA accounts with all the mutual fund companies with whom you intend to invest, and ask the retirement plan to make designated distributions to each of them. For example, if you want to invest half of your money in Fidelity Investment funds and apportion the rest between Vanguard and Janus, you must tell the retirement plan how much to send to each mutual fund.

If you want to take advantage of dollar-cost averaging by gradually funneling your money into investments, you can't ask the retirement plan to dribble out your distribution each month into your selected funds. The best way to dollar-cost average is to ask initially that the money be transferred to a money market fund in the fund family. Then ask the mutual fund family to transfer money each month from the money market fund to the stock and bond funds you have chosen. If you are investing with a brokerage firm or financial planner, they will take responsibility for channeling the money into the appropriate investments at the proper time.

When the time comes to start drawing retirement income from the IRA, you'll want to be sure that the funds are available. For that reason, stash several years' anticipated withdrawals in money market funds or short-term bond funds. That way, if you encounter a bear market, you won't have to sell shares in stock funds or intermediate or long-term bond funds while they are declining in value. You'll be able to draw on the short-term funds while you wait for the markets to turn bullish and begin to increase in value again.

You must begin taking minimum payments from your IRA by April 30 after the year you turn seventy and a half. Upon request, some fund companies will calculate the amount for you and arrange for you to receive regular payments that equal that amount.

If you plan to begin taking distributions immediately, consider an immediate annuity, which will pay you a monthly check for the rest of your life, making it impossible to outlive your money.

Unfortunately, the price you pay for that security is dear: If you die earlier than expected, you will forfeit the rest of your investment. (To avoid this result, you may opt to receive smaller monthly payments in exchange for a guarantee that you or your heirs will receive payments for at least a minimum period, such as ten years.) You'll also find that over the years inflation will erode the buying power of the payments you receive, so be sure to keep an additional nest egg from which you can supplement your annuity payments in later years. If you opt for an immediate annuity, be sure to choose an insurance company with at least an A+ rating from A. M. Best, to ensure that the insurance company is around as long as you are.

Retirement Myths

Much of the current advice about retirement planning is wrong, as it relies on retirement myths left over from the days of our grandparents. Though appropriate for those who felt old when they retired and who died not long thereafter, the myths are inappropriate for today's young-at-heart retiree. Here are some of those retirement myths:

Myth #1. You'll need income for only ten or fifteen years of retirement. The older you get, the more likely you'll live well into your eighties or beyond. When you plan for retirement, count on living to age ninety, or older.

Myth #2. Your primary investment goal is to preserve capital. That may have been true when people lived just a few years into retirement, but not anymore. At only 3 to 4 percent inflation, a sixty-five-year-old retiree will see expenses double by the time he reaches his early eighties. Inflation is your worst enemy in your retirement years, not the risk of market volatility.

Myth #3. You'll need about 70 percent of your current income in retirement. Retirees today are much more active than their earlier counterparts. With lots of extra energy, they can consult or work part-time, making extra money to supplement retirement income, making the money last longer—or else they can travel or engage in expensive hobbies that drain retirement funds. Figure out your *own* retirement income needs, and plan accordingly.

Myth #4. Your income tax bracket will be lower in retirement. Although your income may be less when you retire, don't forget that your itemized deductions and exemptions may also decline, as you pay off the house, go onto Medicare, no longer have employee business expenses, support fewer dependents, or donate less to charity. Overall, you will probably pay the same percentage of your income to taxes that you did during your working years.

Myth #5. Your housing costs will decline. Even in retirement, your property taxes will probably continue to climb. As you age physically, some of the home maintenance tasks you used to do yourself, such as cleaning out the gutters, will need to be done by someone you hire. Even if your house is paid off, you can expect your housing costs to continue to rise.

Myth #6. You'll spend your last years in a nursing home. It is estimated that two out of every five people over sixty-five will spend time in a nursing home—but half of those admitted will stay six months or less, and most of the rest will spend less than three years there. Nursing home coverage, referred to as "long-term care insurance," is very expensive and may not be essential for you.

Myth #7. You should only spend income and never touch principal. The advice "Never touch principal" may have been acceptable for your grandparents, but in today's inflationary world it won't work for you. The income from your investments might be enough to support you today, but that same income will buy considerably less in ten years. For example, if you put $50,000 in a ten-year bond paying 7 percent interest, you'll receive $3,500 a year. But in ten years the buying power of that $3,500 is likely to be cut one-third by inflation, and your bond will be redeemed for only the original $50,000 you invested.

If, on the other hand, you invest $50,000 in a combination of mutual funds that pays only 4 percent a year in current income but grows 7 percent a year, the income from investments will be only $2,000 a year. If you supplement that income by liquidating fund shares and drawing $1,500 from principal each year, you will find that after ten years the value of your fund will have grown to over $75,000. Rather than "Never touch principal," better advice might be "Don't spend all your principal growth."

In retirement, invest for total return and for stability, and don't worry about how much current income your funds are paying. With sufficient total return, you can liquidate shares periodically and your portfolio will still continue to grow. If you need current income, request that fund dividends be paid to you in cash, and liquidate additional shares as necessary. As inflation increases the amount you must withdraw to cover your expenses, eventually your principal value may start to decline. If your principal has grown in the early years of retirement, you will probably still have more than enough to live out your life comfortably. Don't be reluctant to withdraw principal to support your lifestyle in later years, unless your ambition is to live like a pauper so your kids can spend like kings after you are gone.

10

· · · · · · · ·

INVESTING TO SAVE INCOME TAXES

Only death and taxes are inevitable, goes the saying—and at least death doesn't get any worse. Taxes, on the other hand, are increasingly burdensome to many people. The more tax breaks we are promised by Washington, it seems, the greater the burden becomes. This is to be expected, some say, because politicians are in charge of income taxes. Henry Kissinger once said, "Ninety percent of the politicians give the other ten percent a bad reputation."

Investing in retirement plans is the best way to reduce income taxes, because you can deduct your investment from your taxable income and also defer taxes on your investment's growth. But if you are not eligible to contribute to a retirement plan, or if you have invested as much as you can and income taxes are still a concern, investing in some mutual funds can also help you save taxes. Here are two ways to save income taxes on your mutual fund investments:

Tax-free investments. If you invest in municipal bond funds that are tax-free, the dividend income they earn will never be taxed. Tax-free income from municipal bond funds is tax-free on the surface, but is included with other taxable income for some purposes, such as computing minimum taxes or the taxable portion of Social Security benefits. So though the income from municipal bond funds is tax-free, that tax-free income can trigger higher taxes on other income.

Tax-deferred investments. If you invest in tax-deferred investments such as retirement plans, deferred annuities, or variable life insurance, the taxation of principal and/or income is deferred. You will eventually have to pay tax on the money, but meanwhile it grows without annual reduction for taxes. Growth equity funds also provide some tax deferral, because you don't have to pay tax on the appreciation until the underlying stock is sold, or until you sell your shares in the fund.

Municipal Bond Funds

Higher taxes are good for one thing—municipal bond fund sales. Interest from municipal bonds isn't taxed by the federal government, and your state doesn't tax bonds issued within the state. (A few states don't tax the income from any municipal bonds, whether issued within the state or not.) Geographically astute investors can buy municipal bond funds that are double tax-free, or triple tax-free if the bond is free from city taxes as well. There are bond funds that invest exclusively in the bonds of the following states: Alabama, Arizona, California, Colorado, Connecticut, Delaware, Florida, Georgia, Hawaii, Indiana, Kansas, Kentucky, Louisiana, Maine, Maryland, Massachusetts, Michigan, Minnesota, Missouri, New Jersey, New Mexico, New York, North Carolina, North Dakota, Ohio, Oregon, Pennsylvania, South Carolina, Tennessee, Texas, Vermont, Virginia, and West Virginia.

There are two kinds of municipal bond funds: tax-exempt mutual funds and tax-exempt unit trusts. The tax-exempt mutual fund is an open-end fund which accepts new money with which bonds are purchased, and which can buy and sell bonds as needed. The tax-exempt unit trust consists of a fixed portfolio of municipal bonds which it holds until maturity. The fund is closed and will accept no new money, although you can sell your shares in it to someone else on the open market. The fund distributes bond income monthly, and at the bond's maturity it distributes the bond principal to shareholders. When the last bond matures, the fund is dissolved.

If you want to receive monthly bond income, you will find buying municipal bond funds to be superior to direct ownership of the bonds themselves: municipal bonds pay income twice a year, while municipal bond funds pay dividends once a month.

SINGLE-STATE VS. NATIONAL BOND FUNDS

To decide whether to invest in a single-state bond fund or a national bond fund that invests in bonds issued by many states, compare the after-tax return. If the returns are similar, you will sustain less risk with a national fund, because when a state sustains a catastrophe, either financial or natural, it can wreak havoc with the value of single-state bond funds invested in that state. Of course, any bonds of that state that were held in a national bond fund would suffer loss of value as well—but it is unlikely that all the states whose bonds were included in a national portfolio will suffer calamities at the same time. If you are attracted to single-state bond funds, consider funds whose holdings are insured for both income and return of principal.

Are Municipal Bond Funds Right for You?

If municipal bond funds are tax-free, why doesn't everyone buy municipal bonds instead of corporate or U.S. bonds? A major reason is that municipal bonds pay less in interest than other types of bonds, because they don't have to pay higher rates—investors are willing to take a lower interest rate in order to obtain the tax-free income.

When deciding between taxable bond funds and nontaxable municipal bond funds, remember that it isn't what you make that counts, but rather what you keep. If you are in a high tax bracket, municipal bonds will be appropriate for the bond segment of your portfolio. Unfortunately, many people invest in tax-free municipal bonds who are in a lower tax bracket and who would be better off investing in taxable corporate bonds or even in growth stocks. Those folks should remember this maxim: It isn't the taxes you save that count; rather, it's the fund's total return after taxes. Just because an investment is tax-free doesn't mean it will give you the best after-tax return on your investment.

To determine whether tax-free municipal bonds are a good investment for you, first determine whether bonds fit into your asset allocation portfolio (see Chapter 3). Then see whether your tax bracket is high enough that tax reductions make up for the reduced interest rate paid by municipal bonds.

To figure out whether municipal bonds make sense for you, use the following worksheet to calculate the equivalent taxable yield for the municipal bond fund in which you are considering investing.

1. Your combined federal and state tax bracket _____
2. Subtract your tax bracket from 1.00 _____
3. The tax-free yield on your municipal bond fund _____
4. The equivalent taxable yield for your bond fund
   (line 3 divided by line 2) _____

Here is a table to compare the income from a tax-free bond to a taxable investment.

Your Tax Bracket	This tax-exempt yield			
	5%	6%	7%	8%
	Is the equivalent of this taxable yield			
15%	5.9%	7.1%	8.2%	9.4%
28%	6.9%	8.3%	9.7%	11.1%
31%	7.2%	8.7%	10.1%	11.6%
36%	7.8%	9.4%	10.9%	12.5%
39.6%	8.3%	9.9%	11.6%	13.3%

YOUR MUNICIPAL BOND FUND MAY
PRODUCE TAXABLE INCOME

Don't think that every dime you make from a municipal bond fund will be tax-free. If the fund stashes money in an interest-bearing bank account while looking for bonds to buy, your share of the interest earned will be taxable, not exempt. And if the fund sells a bond at a profit, that profit will be taxable to you as capital gains. Finally, if you sell your shares in a municipal bond fund at a profit, your gain will be taxable.

How to Choose Municipal Bond Funds

Don't make the mistake of thinking all bonds are safe. Just as U.S. bonds are guaranteed by the federal government, some municipal bonds, but not all, are guaranteed by the state or municipality that issued them. These are called *general obligation bonds,* and they are backed by the full credit of the issuer. A bit more risky are *revenue bonds,* which are backed by the revenue from whatever project is being built with the money. If the bond finances a new bridge, your interest and eventual principal payoff will come from the tolls people pay to cross the bridge. If the bridge falls down, your bond may collapse as well. If calamity or cost overruns keep the bridge from ever being completed, chances are your bonds will never be paid off.

What other calamities can befall your municipal bonds? Well, the credit rating of the bond may drop, or the municipality may go bankrupt, as did New York City in the 1970s and Orange County, California, in 1994. When a municipality goes bankrupt, its bonds may eventually be paid off in part or in full, or the bondholders may recover nothing at all. Even if the bonds are finally paid in full, the bondholders will have suffered interest defaults. Sometimes economic problems of the issuing municipality will cause the bonds to be downgraded and lose value, even though the municipality doesn't declare bankruptcy. Recently, bonds issued by

California were downgraded because of economic downturns that state suffered in the recession.

As if that weren't enough, municipal bonds are subject to interest rate risk, like all other bonds. If interest rates climb, the value of your bonds will sink no matter who the issuer is. Municipal bonds are often more volatile than other bonds when interest rates are rising.

In addition to the risks inherent in all bond investments—such as interest rate risk, credit risk, inflation risk, and opportunity risk—holders of municipal bonds run the risk that the *tax laws may change.* If tax rates are cut, the tax saved by investing in tax-free municipal bonds will fall as well, reducing the value of the bonds. If other tax laws change and municipal bond income is included in the computation of certain other taxes or of the limitations for certain deductions, that change will reduce the overall benefit of the "tax-free" income.

To pick a bond fund, consider the following:

• *Assess your tolerance for risk.* Long-term bonds fluctuate more than short-term bonds, so recognize that if you seek the higher yields of long-term bonds you'll have to accept the higher volatility.

• *Consider both the yield and the total return.* If your high-interest-rate bond falls in value, you'll make less than you would have if you had invested more conservatively. Intermediate bond funds are generally far less volatile than long-term bond funds.

• *Consider the credit ratings of the bonds in the mutual fund.* All bonds are not the same, and the lower-rated bonds could have default problems in a faltering economy. Consider lower-rated bond funds only if you are willing to accept greater risks in order to speculate on greater returns.

• *Consider the prepayment risk.* Your bond may offer a dandy return, but if it can be redeemed within a few years, that return may not last for long—if the bond issuer decides to redeem the bond and pay your fund off. Typically, this happens when interest rates have declined, so you won't be able to reinvest the payoff you receive in a bond paying similar interest.

• *Look at your tax situation.* If you are in a tax bracket of 28 percent or more, you may be better off buying a municipal bond fund than a taxable bond fund. Use the worksheet on page 126 to make this computation.

• *Look at the fund's expense ratio.* This is particularly important for bond funds, because they don't appreciate in value as stock funds do, so a high expense ratio will really eat into your total return. The bond funds offered by the Vanguard Group generally have very low expense ratios.

Some municipal bond funds hold insured bonds, whose interest and principal are guaranteed by an insurance company. If the municipal bond defaults, you can look to the insurance company for payment. In some cases, the bond is originally issued with the insurance coverage, paid for by the municipality that issued it. In other cases, the fund itself purchases insurance to cover the bonds held in the portfolio. Before you decide to invest in a fund that is insured, compare the yields with those of an uninsured portfolio of high-grade municipal bonds. The cost of insurance coverage generally will reduce the yield by .25 to .50 of a percent. You may decide in favor of the higher yield if high-grade municipal bonds provide sufficient safety for your peace of mind. On the other hand, if you desire reassurance, the insured bond fund will be worth the slightly diminished return.

Diversification is particularly important in municipal bonds. For safety's sake, and stability as well, it is important to spread your investment across a wide range of creditworthy bonds with varying maturities. Because municipal bonds are just one segment of most investors' portfolios, it is difficult to attain the necessary diversification by holding individual bonds. That is why many investors turn to municipal bond funds, which offer wide diversification, professional management, and high liquidity.

Municipal bonds are rated by Standard & Poor's and Moody's. The bonds rated AAA are of the highest credit. AA- and A-rated bonds are also considered to be investment grade. BBB-rated bonds are at the lowest end of investment grade. The rest of the B ratings (BB and B) are speculative, as are all the Cs (CCC, CC, and C). D-rated bonds are already in default.

Surprisingly, municipal bond funds comprised of AAA-rated bonds may not give you the best protection against credit risk. If the bond rating changes, there is only one way for the rating to go—down. Lower-rated bonds whose prospects might improve could have their rating increased while your bond fund holds them. If that happens, the value of the bond will increase as well, even though interest rates have not changed.

Good management is crucial for good performance from a municipal bond fund. The fund must find the right bonds, buy them at the right price, and eventually sell them into the market judiciously.

Compare Apples with Apples When Choosing Bond Funds

When comparing tax-free municipal bond funds with taxable bond funds, don't just consider the relative yield between tax-free funds and taxable bond funds. Credit risk is very important as well. A bond fund comprised entirely of U.S. Treasury obligations is preferable to a highly rated municipal bond fund that yields the same after-tax return, because U.S. Treasury bonds are of higher credit quality than the top-rated municipal bonds. However, if the municipal bonds are insured, the quality of the municipal bond fund will be nearly equivalent to that of the U.S. Treasury bond fund. If the municipal bonds are not insured, they would probably best be compared to a top-rated corporate bond of an equivalent maturity.

The type of municipal bond also makes a difference. A general obligation municipal bond would likely be of higher quality than a top-rated corporate bond, but other types of municipal bonds would be similar in quality to the corporate bonds.

Don't forget that while the ordinary income from the fund is taxfree, the capital gains are not. If interest rates decline sharply, much of the return from the fund will come from capital gains, and those capital gains will be fully taxable.

Variable Annuities

What do you get when you cross an insurance policy with a family of mutual funds? A *variable annuity*. If you want to invest in mutual funds but you don't want to pay tax on the earnings or growth each year, a variable annuity may be a good investment for you. A variable annuity is an insurance product that lets you invest your money in "subaccounts" that function just like mutual funds. As a matter of fact, the subaccounts are often run by well-known mutual fund companies. Variable annuities are good for high-tax-bracket long-term investors.

The primary benefit of investing in variable annuities is the tax-deferred compounding. Obviously, the longer your money will stay in the annuity, the greater that benefit will be, so consider a variable annuity for your Striver portfolio, not for Conserver or Builder portfolios. Additional benefits of variable annuities include an unlimited investment ceiling (in contrast to IRAs and other retirement plans), a wide variety of investment funds available, and a death-benefit guarantee.

Disadvantages of variable annuities include higher fees, surrender charges, and tax penalties for removing money prematurely. In addition to the regular mutual fund management expenses, there are several other fees associated with variable annuities. Because the annuity is issued by an insurance company, there are insurance-related charges, called mortality and expense-risk charges. These charges range from .5 to 1.5 percent, and average 1.26 percent. The annuity will also have an annual contract maintenance fee of $25 to $50, and a surrender charge, typically 5 to 8 percent, that disappears once you've held the annuity for six to eleven years. You will be charged the surrender fee only if you cash in the annuity, and many annuities allow you to withdraw up to 10 percent of the value of the annuity each year without paying a surrender fee. If you take your money out of the annuity before you are fifty-nine and a half, you'll also owe the IRS a 10 percent penalty on the earnings. And although the earnings of an annuity are sheltered from current taxation, the money you put into the plan is not tax-deductible, as is money invested in a retirement plan.

The performance of variable annuities is tracked in Morningstar's "Variable Annuity/Life Performance Report," and occasionally in some of the financial magazines. When you compare variable annuities, look at the performance of the mutual fund subaccounts, and at the fees, just as you would with any mutual fund. This information can be found in an annuity's prospectus. You can buy annuities through stockbrokers, financial planners, insurance agents, and some large mutual fund companies such as Dreyfus, Fidelity, T. Rowe Price, Scudder, and Vanguard.

Death-Benefit Guarantees
With death-benefit guarantees, annuities provide a way you can invest in the stock market without risking your principal. The annuity guarantees that if you die, the total amount that the annuity pays to your heirs will be at least as much as you invested originally, less any amount you've already withdrawn.

Many annuities allow a step-up of the guarantee every five or seven years to the then-current market value, and some guarantee a certain return on your investments, usually 5 percent. Remember three things about the death-benefit guarantees: You have to die before it becomes operative, so it won't protect you if you cash in your annuity during your lifetime; the expenses are higher to pay for these guarantees, and so your total return will be less; and the insurance company offering the annuity must outlive you for your heirs to collect their benefit, so be sure the company is rated A+ or better by A. M. Best.

VARIABLE ANNUITIES FOR BARGAIN HUNTERS
The least expensive variable annuities on the market are the Vanguard Group Variable Annuity and the Scudder Horizon Plan through Charter National Life Insurance Co. Vanguard uses National Home Life

Assurance Co. for its annuity offering, and the total cost is less than
1 percent. The cost of the Scudder annuity is 1.36 percent.

The Phases of Annuities

Though the term *annuity* makes us think of "income for life," that
concept of annuities is a little old-fashioned. Annuities typically
have two phases, the *accumulation phase* and the *payout* or *distribution phase*. It is the accumulation phase that is the focus of today's
benefits of investing in annuities.

An annuity in the accumulation phase is called a *deferred annuity*.
During this accumulation phase, you make an initial investment
and may add additional funds to the annuity periodically. The
annuity makes no current payments to you, and its earnings are
reinvested. The earnings are not subject to current income tax, as
long as they remain within the annuity. In addition, the annuity
has a small death benefit, which guarantees that if you die, your
beneficiary will receive at least as much as you have invested, even
if the value of your investments has declined.

An annuity in which you begin receiving payments immediately
is called an *immediate annuity*. In the payout phase of an annuity,
you can choose to take a lump-sum payout, or to take a series of
payments. If you choose the series of payments, they can be of a
fixed amount for a set number of years, or a fixed amount for your
lifetime or the joint lifetimes of yourself and another beneficiary,
such as your spouse. If you choose the guaranteed lifetime payments, you have the option of adding an optional "period certain," which provides that payments will continue for a specified
period even if you should die sooner. For example, assume payments are to continue for your lifetime, but for a period certain of
at least ten years. If you die after eight years, your beneficiaries will
receive payments for two more years. If you live for more than ten
years, your beneficiaries will receive nothing, because the payout
during your lifetime exceeded the period certain.

Before you buy an annuity, check the insurance company's rating in A. M. Best, Standard & Poor's, or Moody's to make sure it

has a top rating. Though that doesn't guarantee that the company is in prime financial health, it should be a good indicator of its strength. Look at the money manager's track record and history. Many annuity funds that are offered by mutual fund companies, such as Fidelity or Vanguard, use money managers who also manage similar funds within their mutual fund portfolio, so you can check the track records of those mutual funds as well to get a sense of the manager's abilities.

Compare the fees of the various annuities you are considering. Although you won't just pick the annuity with the lowest fees, likewise you won't want to consider only performance, without considering fees at all. Also compare surrender fees—though if you choose your annuity carefully, you will probably not surrender the annuity within the six to eleven years during which the surrender fee typically applies.

If you invest in a fixed annuity, which earns a specified percentage return each year, be aware that the money you turn over to the insurance company becomes a part of their general account. If the insurance company has financial troubles down the road, your money can go to the insurance company's creditors rather than to you. Be particularly careful when selecting a company, and select only those with ratings of A+ or higher by A. M. Best or Standard & Poor's.

You needn't be as concerned about the credit rating of the insurance company with whom you invest money into a variable annuity. In variable annuities, your money is invested in a separate account that is beyond the reach of the insurance company's general creditors.

You can review the performance of variable annuities in the annual Morningstar *Variable Annuity Sourcebook,* which is available at larger libraries and at the offices of many brokers and financial planners.

Penalties for Dumping Your Annuity
To discourage you from bailing out of annuities prematurely, the IRS charges you a 10 percent penalty, and income taxes to boot, on

all earnings you withdraw from an annuity before you are fifty-nine and a half. However, this does not mean you are locked into an annuity forever. If you are unhappy with your annuity, you may exchange it for another annuity without paying the 10 percent IRS penalty or current income taxes on the earnings. This is called a Section 1035 exchange. Be aware, however, that a Section 1035 transfer may still be subject to stiff surrender charges imposed by the insurance company for early withdrawal. However, most annuities allow you to remove up to 10 percent of the annuity's value or of your initial investment (whichever is greater) each year without paying a surrender charge.

Comparing Annuities

When deciding whether a variable annuity is right for you, project the amount that you would have in the variable annuity a number of years in the future, and compare this with the results you could achieve with a similar group of investments in mutual funds. You can then decide if it makes sense on a comparative-return basis. If you plan to invest for less than ten years, you will probably find that the extra charges layered into the variable annuity reduce the overall return to such an extent that the tax deferral simply makes no sense. If you will hold the annuity for longer than ten years, the advantage of the deferral of income taxes generally will overcome the higher cost of the annuity.

Universal Variable Life Insurance

Universal variable life insurance is like whole life insurance, except you can make investments within the contract in funds that resemble mutual funds. With universal variable life, you can vary your premium payments, increasing or decreasing the insurance protection and cash value growth of the policy by paying more in some years and cutting back when you need to. That is a great benefit for those whose cash flow varies, and who don't want to obligate themselves to a large fixed investment commitment. You can also borrow against the funds, and the money you withdraw will be tax-free. In addition, since you are borrowing against your policy's cash value, you never need to pay the loan back (you will pay annual interest, however).

The lure of universal variable life policies is great—they combine a death benefit with a tax-sheltered investment plan. The drawback of variable life insurance can be summed up in one word: *fees*. A considerable amount of the premiums you pay goes toward commissions and ongoing life insurance coverage. Universal variable life policies provide a stunning return—for the insurance agent or broker who sells you the policy. The costs associated with universal variable life policies are very high, and may zap the benefits you hoped to derive from tax-deferred returns.

Expect fees to average about 25 percent of the premiums you pay. If you need life insurance anyway, that may be an acceptable fee for the combination of life insurance and tax-sheltered investment. But if you have no need for life insurance, the additional fees involved may eat up the tax savings involved.

ALTERNATIVES TO VARIABLE LIFE POLICIES

Ordinary universal life policies pay interest at a fixed rate established each year by the insurance company. Variable universal life policies let you allocate your investments among the insurance-company-sponsored mutual funds. The cost of a regular universal life policy is considerably less, often less than half, which means you might be better off accepting the lower rate of return for less in premiums. Or you might even go for term insurance, and invest the rest in investments that don't carry exorbitant fees.

Check the features of variable life as you would any other insurance investment: verify the viability of the insurance company in one of the publications of the insurance rating companies; understand the surrender fees and front loads; and analyze the returns on investments for the underlying mutual funds, by comparing them with the performance of similar funds that are not part of a variable insurance portfolio.

If you invest in an annuity or variable life product, be sure to pick the insurance company carefully. Insist on an A+ rating from A. M. Best, or a AAA rating from Standard & Poor's or Moody's Investor Services. You want to make sure that the insurance company is around as long as you are.

Because of large up-front costs, plan to hold a universal variable life policy for at least ten years, because it will likely take that long for the investment returns to make up for the commissions and fees. As with other life insurance policies, you can borrow against the cash value, with any outstanding loans deducted from the insurance benefit at your death. If you hold the policy until you die, that means that you will have use of the money you borrow without ever having to pay tax on any of the earnings, which is a considerable tax advantage over ordinary mutual fund investments.

Stock Index Funds Save Taxes Too

Stock index funds invest in the same stocks that make up a particular index, such as the S&P 500. Although most people don't think of stock index funds when they think of tax-deferred investments, stock index funds offer four big breaks over many tax-deferred investments:

- *They are low-cost.* You'll pay far less for a stock index fund than you will for a variable annuity. The average annual expense of a stock index fund is .35 percent. The average comparable annuity charges .43 percent in expenses plus insurance charges of 1.25 percent—a total of 1.68 percent, which is almost five times as much.
- *Stock index funds buy and hold, rather than buying and selling stocks actively.* That means that if the fund averages a 10 percent return, of which 3 percent comes from dividends and the rest from stock price increases, only 3 percent of it will be currently taxable. The rest will be tax-deferred, just as with a variable annuity or a nondeductible IRA.
- *When you sell your shares in the stock index fund, you'll pay tax at*

capital gains rates, currently a maximum of 28 percent. This is a boon for an investor whose ordinary income tax rate is higher than that. The income from variable annuities and nondeductible IRAs is taxed at ordinary income tax rates.

• *When you die, the stock index fund will receive a stepped-up basis to its value on the date of your death.* Because only the difference between the sales price and that new tax basis is taxable, your heirs will not have to pay tax on the growth when they sell it. This isn't true of your variable annuities or IRAs—their earnings will be taxed to your heirs.

The investments discussed in this chapter won't eliminate your income taxes, but they will eliminate or defer the taxes on your investment earnings and growth. Before you opt for the income tax benefits of these investments, be sure that your tax bracket is high enough to warrant them. Remember, there is always a trade-off for the tax benefits, either in terms of reduced yield or greater expenses. Be sure you will receive full benefit from the tax advantage before you accept the reduced income or additional costs.

11

· · · · · · · ·

GETTING PROFESSIONAL ADVICE

In this book, you have learned to create your own portfolio of
mutual funds and to use the worksheets to monitor your investments and rebalance periodically. But even with what you've
learned, you may still feel you don't have the competence, confidence, or time to research funds, read prospectuses, and make
your own investments and monitor them.

You may need professional help to get you moving and staying
on track. Just as some people dieting do better in a diet program or
with a diet coach or group than on their own, so do many invest
better when they have a professional with whom they can counsel.
A financial adviser can help keep you on track and stay invested
when your natural inclination is to cut and run. Statistics show that
the average length of time an investor holds shares in a no-load
fund is seventeen months, while investors in load funds, which are
mostly sold through financial advisers, keep their money in the
fund for forty-eight months. The longer you stay invested in a fund,
the more likely you are to reap the potential rewards of positive
fund performance, and a financial adviser can help bolster your
resolve, enhancing financial returns.

Some investors simply don't have the time to devote to monitoring their investments; others lack the discipline to follow through;
and still others tend to get carried away on a tide of emotions, picking "hot" funds when the market is rising without regard for proper

allocation, and selling in a panic when prices drop. If any of this applies to you, you will probably benefit from the services of a qualified, ethical stockbroker, financial planner, or money manager.

When deciding whether you need to consult a professional, consider your knowledge of investing and how much time you are prepared to dedicate to researching funds and monitoring your investments. No-load mutual fund buyers spend many more hours researching mutual funds than do investors who rely upon brokers and financial advisers. Ignore your neighbor who invests in no-loads and says you'd be a fool to use a broker. In 1990, about 70 percent of all mutual fund investors bought their funds through a professional at a brokerage house, bank, or insurance company. They did so because they wanted and needed advice regarding their investments.

Every professional is compensated in one way or another, so hiring a professional will be somewhat more expensive than going it alone. But if a professional can dissuade you from panic selling after a market dip, just before the market turns a corner and heads back upward, or can encourage you to stick to your basic plan of asset allocation when times are bad, the cost of the professional advice will be negligible compared to the money you will earn by making the right decisions.

Don't Be Duped
When you seek professional help with your portfolio, the knowledge you have acquired about mutual funds and your own financial profile will help you communicate more effectively and intelligently with your chosen adviser, so that you will better be able to meet your financial goals. Your new knowledge will also help you steer clear of financial professionals who are incompetent, or who don't have your best interests in mind.

Review what you've learned in this book. If the financial professional's advice seems consistent with everything you've learned, the two of you are in sync and on the right track. If the professional's advice seems entirely contradictory to what you've learned, or if important details, such as risks, are being glossed over, you may be dealing with the wrong person. With your newfound knowledge, you won't be in danger of being talked into the wrong mutual funds by a glib broker with only his own interests in mind. Remember that the ultimate decision to invest always lies with you.

If you are uncertain about the investment advice you are receiving, review your goals once more, and review the recommended asset mix for your financial profile. Each financial professional will model his or her recommended portfolio somewhat differently, but they should generally be in line. It's like shopping for clothing: although the style and cut of garments will differ somewhat depending on the manufacturer, the size and type of garments will be similar. If a salesman tries to sell you an extra-large shirt when you normally wear medium, or if he pushes you toward a gauzy garment when you need a winter coat, you know he isn't paying attention to your needs. The same is true of financial professionals. Emphasize your concerns, and if they aren't addressed adequately, don't invest.

MAINTAIN YOUR BALANCE

Remember, proper asset allocation accounts for 92 percent of investment returns, according to studies. Once you've picked the asset allocation that suits your goals, it is important to maintain that allocation by rebalancing your portfolio frequently. For example, when the stock market has been enjoying a rapid bull run upward, but the bond market has lagged behind, it is time to transfer some of your money from equity funds to bond funds and rebalance. (See pages 82–83.) That makes sense intellectually, yet when faced with selling equity funds that have risen dramatically in the past few months, your gut tells you no. Why leave the party just when everyone has really begun to have fun? The answer, of course, is that the party could end abruptly quite soon, so you should take some of your profits and move them to the site of the next party before the party gets under way there. A financial professional can help you find the next party, and can encourage you to action when you are inclined to procrastinate.

Load Funds

If you buy a load mutual fund, an initial sales charge, called a load, will be deducted before your money is invested in the fund. (See Chapter 4 for a discussion of loads and fees.) Although the load can be as high as 8.5 percent, the loads charged today commonly range between 4 and 6 percent.

Load funds are sold through stockbrokers, financial planners, banks, and insurance agents, who are compensated from the load for having sold you the fund. The portion of the load that does not go to the salesperson goes into the coffers of the company the salesperson represents. If you bought the fund directly from the mutual fund company, the company keeps the load.

When loads were high, no-load funds had a distinct advantage over 8.5 percent load funds. But with loads now averaging 4 percent, and many even less, the advantage is not so great. Although paying a 4 percent load up front reduces the total return you will receive, over a number of years the impact of that load will decline dramatically. For example, if you hold the fund for one year, your total return will be reduced 4 percent. But if you hold the fund for four years, the impact will average just 1 percent per year. You generally can reduce the amount of load by investing more with the company initially, or by signing a letter of intent pledging to invest more money into that fund or a related fund within thirteen months. For example, if the regular load is 4 percent, you may end up paying less if you invest more than $100,000. And if you invest more than $1 million, you may pay nothing at all. Look at the fund prospectus to see what the breakpoints are.

DON'T PAY TO REINVEST DIVIDENDS

A few fund groups, such as Franklin and Mass. Financial, charge their shareholders for reinvesting dividends. Obviously, there is no sales cost to the company to reinvest your dividends. Fortunately, the practice of charging a sales charge on reinvested dividends is dying. If you own shares in a fund that levies such a charge, you would be better off taking your dividends in cash and investing them in a no-load fund.

Back-Load Funds

Most people think of front loads when they think of loads. But a fund may instead have a back load, which is charged when you sell the fund. Some funds have both. Back loads work just like front loads, except they are charged on the value of your fund (not just your initial investment) when you sell it. Some fund families have dropped the front load for some of their funds in favor of a disappearing back load, known as a contingent deferred sales load (CDSL). For example, the fund might charge you a 4 percent fee if you redeemed your shares within one year of purchasing them, 3 percent if you redeemed in the second year, etc. Funds that charge a disappearing back load usually charge an annual 12b-1 fee as well, often as much as 1 percent per year. So if you hold your shares for four years, you still will have paid a 4 percent fee, at the rate of 1 percent a year, even though you paid no front or back load. To mitigate this problem, some funds cap the load at 6 percent (or some other percentage), exchanging your shares into an identical fund that has no 12b-1 fee as soon as you have reached the fee ceiling.

Some funds have redemption fees, typically 1 to 2 percent, that disappear after a year. Redemption fees are imposed to deter short-term trading, which is very expensive for the fund in terms of processing costs. Some funds have small "exit fees" of .25 percent or so to cover the cost of paperwork. These fees are often payable to the fund itself, and therefore increase the remaining shareholders' fund profits, rather than going to the management company.

Dual Pricing: Choosing the Best Plan for You

Some funds offer dual pricing, creating two classes of shares for each fund: A-shares have a front-end load, and B-shares have a back load combined with a 12b-1 fee. That gives you a choice: pay a front-end load, or pay a 12b-1 fee. Don't be fooled by the relative fund performances into choosing one over the other. The published fund performance reflects the cost of the 12b-1 fee, but doesn't reflect the front-load or back-load costs. Once you subtract those fees, particularly for short-term investors, the performance of the fund could be reduced considerably. For example, a fund charging a 5 percent front load may have a total return of 6 percent, while a similar fund charging a 1 percent 12b-1 fee has a total return of 5 percent. The performance of the two funds is virtually identical, but the performance for the front-load fund hasn't been reduced for the front-end load, while the 12b-1 fee has already been deducted from the reported performance of the other fund. If you keep the fund for five years, your performance results will be virtually the same. If you keep the fund for less than five years, you will probably make more with the 12b-1 fund, even though the other fund reports better performance. If you stay invested for more than five years, the front-load fund will probably produce superior long-term results.

Front-load fees won't impact fund returns for a long-term investor nearly as much as for a short-term investor, as the cost of the load will be diluted by years of investment performance. In addition, most back-load fees are disappearing, so a long-term investor will never pay those fees. Some funds nowadays cap the 12b-1 fee at the amount you would have paid had you purchased the fund with a front load. This means loads and 12b-1 fees should be of far less concern to the long-term investor than to the short-term investor. Even investors who move from fund to fund, but who will have their money invested for a long period of time, can avoid recurring load by moving their money within the same family of funds.

CAN YOU BUY DIRECT AND AVOID THE LOAD?

You can't avoid a load by buying load funds directly from the mutual fund company. If you are going to buy load funds, you will be better off doing so through a commissioned stockbroker or financial adviser, so you can receive some ongoing financial advice for your money.

The Pros and Cons
of Load Funds

Why Buy a Load Fund?

Why would you ever buy a load fund, when you could buy a no-load? The answer is easy: For the service involved. The sales representative who sells you the load fund is there to advise you, help you define your investment objectives, answer your questions, help you select the funds that are best for you, and to troubleshoot if you have any problems while you own the fund. With a no-load fund, you will make your own decisions, deal directly with the mutual fund company, sort through the prospectus, fill out your own documents, and interface with the mutual fund company yourself. You won't get any personal investment advice from the mutual fund company about which fund is best for you. That's fine if you don't need advice, and feel competent to make your own investment decisions. But as with do-it-yourself auto mechanics, if you don't know what you are doing, you might want to rely on a professional and pay the extra costs.

Don't let a load keep you from relying on a professional for advice. A 4 or 5 percent fee paid up front in exchange for years of advice and service is a real bargain. Over time, the impact of that load will matter less and less.

Don't let a load stand between you and the best possible fund for you. Some load funds consistently perform better than most no-load funds, so don't fail to consider a fund just because it charges a load. But loads don't buy better performance; they are sales charges used to compensate the person who sold you the fund, not the manager who runs it. The fee pays for the advice of the broker, which may be important to you if you want to rely on an expert.

WHEN TO BUY A LOAD FUND

In 1970, less than 10 percent of mutual funds were no-load, and most load funds levied sales charges of 8 percent or more. Today only 60 percent of common stock funds are load funds, and none of the money market funds charge a load. In general, the more stable a fund's return and the more its fortunes are dictated by market movements and interest rates rather than by actions of the portfolio manager, the less incentive you have for buying a load fund. In actuality, a load in no way guarantees that a fund's manager has superior stock-picking abilities, so you should probably buy a load fund only if you need the professional help of the commissioned salesperson who recommends it to you, or if the fund has a history of high performance unmatched by any no-load fund.

When Should You Avoid a Load?

If you are investing for a short period of time, load becomes very important, and you are probably better off with a no-load fund. But if you are investing in the fund for several years, then the load becomes less important, and selecting a fund with good performance is of far greater importance whether it is load or no-load. Paying a moderate load for a fund with superior past performance is far better than just investing in any old no-load.

When you invest in bonds, avoid paying a load if you can. Because the value of bonds doesn't grow like that of growth stocks, in bond funds it won't be as easy to recoup the money you spent on a load as it will be with growth stock funds. Most short-term bond funds maintain similar portfolios, so it doesn't make sense to pay a high load for a short-term bond fund unless it is an integral part of a package designed for you by an investment adviser or stockbroker who deserves to be compensated for his or her time.

DOES A LOAD BUY BETTER PERFORMANCE?

A load fund won't necessarily perform any better (or worse) than a no-load fund. Mutual fund performance isn't dependent on whether you paid a load or not. The stock market doesn't know or care whether you paid a fee to buy into the fund, or whether you will pay a fee during the time that you own it or when you sell it.

Do No-Load Funds Have Higher Expenses?

Some brokers who sell load funds say that no-load funds have higher expense ratios than load funds. But studies show that only a handful of no-load funds charge more than load funds.

Remember that the front loads are not taken into account when total returns are calculated for the funds, so you must make your own adjustment when comparing load funds to no-load mutual funds. The SEC has made this job somewhat easier by requiring each mutual fund to include a table in its prospectus calculating the fund's annual operating costs and the impact of the front load on fund investors who hold their shares for one, three, five, and ten years.

All About Financial Planners

Financial planners come in many shapes and sizes, and have various qualifications as well. Almost anyone can call himself a financial planner, no matter how slim his qualifications. Planners who carry a CFP designation have received the Certified Financial Planner certificate from the College for Financial Planning, which is a self-study program with a comprehensive exam. The ChFC designation is a similar program, generally with an emphasis on insurance products, granted by the American College. Although these designations show that the planner has completed some courses, they still don't tell you whether the planner is good or bad, or whether, even if the planner is good, he or she is the right planner for you.

The International Association for Financial Planning publishes an annual *Registry of Financial Planning*, which is a directory of planners who meet certain educational and experience requirements. To obtain a copy of the registry, send $2.50 to IAFP

Customer Relations, Two Concourse Parkway, Suite 800, Atlanta, GA 30328.

Your Relationship with Your Investment Adviser

If you decide to employ a stockbroker or financial planner, find one with whom you feel compatible. Once you find the right adviser, you will probably stay with that person for many years, and that person will share with you the ups and downs of your life over the years. Working with someone concerned with your goals, your aspirations, and your money will create a very intimate bond.

If you use an investment adviser, the relationship will mature over time, as you reveal your financial situation and goals, and as your life changes over the years. Some people don't want to reveal information about their financial life, and for them the investment adviser–client relationship won't work well. They may be better off making investments on their own, unless they can reconcile themselves to the prospect of revealing details of their financial circumstances and goals.

Buying Mutual Funds Through Insurance Agents

Insurance agents are also sometimes called financial planners, because many insurance products now heavily emphasize investment aspects, and combine insurance with mutual funds to provide both life insurance and fund investments.

Many insurance companies have set up their own mutual funds. If you buy mutual funds through the agent for a large company, your selection will generally be limited to the funds offered by that company. Some of those funds are quite good, while the performance of others has been mediocre. Independent insurance agents may be able to offer you a variety of mutual funds from several different companies.

In the past, most of the mutual funds offered by insurance companies were sold as part of a retirement plan, annuity, or other insurance product. For example, if you set up a profit-sharing plan with the insurance company, you would invest a portion of the profit-sharing plan's money into mutual funds sold by the insurance company. As the distinctions between various financial professionals continue to blur, insurance agents are beginning to offer more mutual fund products directly to the general public. If you are offered investment advice by an insurance agent, be sure that he or she is well versed in the fundamentals of asset allocation. If the insurance agent does not have much experience analyzing various mutual funds, you may want to obtain a second opinion before you invest.

Buying Mutual Funds Through Banks

Banks, too, have climbed aboard the financial planning bandwagon. When interest rates began dropping in the early 1980s, funds began to flow out of banks and into mutual funds. Anxious to keep the business, many banks made mutual funds available to their customers, and some banks have actually established their own line of mutual funds.

Although you can buy mutual funds through your bank, there are generally far fewer choices available from banks than from other financial sources. Banks originally sold a limited range of high-load funds, but recently they have expanded the range of funds available and reduced the loads. Now some larger banks offer bank-sponsored funds, some of which—for example, the Stagecoach Funds sponsored by Wells Fargo Bank—perform quite well when compared with similar-type funds offered by mutual fund companies. Most of the funds sponsored and promoted by banks are lower in volatility; primarily they are bond and growth and income funds. Annuities are quite popular with banks, who market them as "CD alternatives."

If you are considering a bank-sponsored fund, be sure to check the expenses. Surprisingly, the best fund may not be the one with the lowest expense ratio. Although you don't want to choose the fund with the highest expenses, be suspicious of a fund with abnormally low expenses. When funds start out and investments are small, the expenses are often high in relation to the amount invested, and so the expense ratio will be high. A high expense ratio means lower performance, and investors may be slow to pour money into a fund whose performance is depressed. To get their funds going, many banks have subsidized the funds by absorbing a chunk of their expenses during the early years. This boosts performance and makes a fund more attractive—but you should realize that this subsidy won't continue forever. Before you invest, be sure the fund's expenses *before* the subsidy are in line with those of similar funds. That way, when the bank reduces or eliminates its subsidy, the fund will be able to stand alone and continue to provide satisfactory performance.

How Financial Planners Are Compensated

Financial planners are compensated in a variety of ways. A few planners charge an hourly fee and receive no commissions from the investments you make. Some collect both fees and commissions, and some of these will offset the commissions they collect against fees they charge, so you don't pay twice. Other financial professionals charge a fee that is a percentage of the money they manage for you, typically between 1 and 3 percent. Other professionals, such as stockbrokers, are paid only commissions; they are compensated from the load on mutual funds you buy.

Although all planners should have your best interests in mind, some people believe that fee-based planners, who are either paid for their time or who benefit more when your investments increase, are less biased than planners who are paid commissions for the investment products they sell you. Fortunately for the public, this is not necessarily true. There are many good commission-based financial planners and stockbrokers who are honest and objective, and who carefully consider their clients' needs when making portfolio recommendations.

CHECK YOUR ADVISER'S RECORD

When choosing a financial adviser, be sure the professional has a clean record. You can call your state securities department and the federal Securities and Exchange Commission in Washington ([202] 272-7450) to see if the financial adviser has been subjected to disciplinary actions or investigation. If the adviser is part of a National Association of Securities Dealers (NASD)–member firm, you can call the NASD ([800] 289-9999) to see if there are any disciplinary actions pending or judgments rendered against him or her.

Questions to Ask When Choosing an Adviser

To choose a financial professional, ask friends, family, and other professionals for recommendations. Then interview several of the most highly recommended advisers.

When choosing an investment adviser, here are some of the questions to ask:

How long have you been in business? You'll want someone with plenty of experience, who has operated in bear markets as well as bull markets. That means someone who has been a financial adviser for at least six years, or has extensive investment experience.

What type of clients do you serve? If you are a young, aggressive investor, you probably won't do well with a broker who specializes in serving retirees, and vice versa. Most financial advisers serve a variety of clients, so that won't be a problem.

If you have very little money, you probably won't get enough attention from an adviser whose clients are very wealthy, and if you have a great deal of money, you won't want an adviser who is unused to handling large investments.

How often will I talk to you? Look for an adviser who wants to meet with you on a regular basis, perhaps quarterly, to discuss your account. Find an adviser who will give you quality time as well as a quantity of time. As you interview the adviser, you will get a feel for how willing he or she is to explain investments to you, and how well he or she communicates. Choose someone who seems interested in you and your investments, not just your money.

On the other hand, you don't want an adviser who gives you more information than you can stomach, bombarding you with minute technical details regarding funds' attributes. And unless you are lonely or particularly gregarious, you probably don't want an adviser who calls you constantly. That indicates that the adviser doesn't have enough to do and may try to trade you in and out of investments to increase frequency of commissions.

How much will you make? The adviser should be willing to disclose his or her fees and commissions. Don't balk because there are commissions—it's the normal way brokers are compensated—but beware of brokers who place you exclusively in funds that have 8.5 percent sales charges, the maximum allowed by law. Most brokers are ethical, and will steer you toward funds with lower loads overall, and reduced fees for larger investments, if you qualify for them.

Ask the adviser whether there is a sales contest or other sales incentive program that involves the investments he or she is recommending to you. Sometimes vacation packages or other goodies are promised to brokers by their firms, or by the mutual fund companies themselves, if they sell enough of a certain investment.

Can you show me a typical client's performance for the past few years? Let the adviser blank out the names of his clients to preserve their privacy, then review the performance. Ask the adviser to compare that performance to appropriate yardsticks, such as the S&P 500.

Also ask the adviser for the names of three of his or her clients whose financial goals resemble yours. Call those clients and ask about their degree of satisfaction with the adviser's services and their portfolios' performance results.

What do you need to know about me? The adviser should ask a lot of questions about your income, your financial goals, and your investment experience, and should probe for details to assess your tolerance for volatility. The adviser should take notes, and listen more than he or she talks. The more details the adviser requests from you, the more closely his or her recommendations are likely to match your needs.

If you don't feel comfortable with a particular broker, financial adviser, or insurance agent, move on. Ask friends and other professionals for recommendations, and interview them all. Ask for their credentials and track records, and request references. Talk to them about your situation and weigh their recommendations against each other, and against what you've learned in this book. The right choice will become apparent.

NO-LOAD MANAGERS

Some financial planners invest your money in no-loads, and then charge you a fee, ranging from 1 to 2 percent each year, to manage the portfolio. If you are investing for several years, you might be better off investing in load funds through a commission-based planner or stockbroker. For example, a managed portfolio that costs 1 percent per year will cost 10 percent over ten years—based on the current value of the portfolio, not just the amount originally invested. This is likely to be much more than the load charged on a similar portfolio bought from a stockbroker. On the other hand, if you are convinced that the manager provides considerable added value that your stockbroker does not, in terms of growth and investment expertise, you may not mind paying the annual management fee.

Mutual Fund Newsletters

There are many mutual fund newsletters on the market, and each one takes a somewhat different approach to investing. Some newsletters are devoted entirely to advising you on the funds offered by a particular family of funds, such as Fidelity or Vanguard. Other newsletters promote market timing, urging you to move from one type of investment to another at certain times. Some newsletters analyze fund managers, while others focus on risk tolerance and investment goals for various types of investors.

At the end of 1992 there were 135 newsletters in existence, at a typical cost of $150 per year. Yet in a study by *The Hulbert Financial Digest,* only three of the thirty-six advisers in operation for the full ten years from 1983 to 1992 outpaced the unmanaged index of the total stock market. Although many of the newsletters were able to advise subscribers to get out of the market before a big dip, twenty-nine newsletters missed advising their subscribers to get back in at the appropriate time. As a consequence, those subscribers often reinvested at prices that were higher than the prices at which they sold. They would have been better off as buy-and-hold investors, waiting out the dip, rather than selling their investments and later reinvesting at higher prices.

Most newsletter subscribers are not disciplined enough to follow the newsletters' instructions promptly and explicitly, month after month. Those investors are like Dolly Parton, who once said of Jane Fonda's exercise video, "I could sit on the sofa all day long eating popcorn and watching that gal jump around." So too, most newsletter readers do so for recreation rather than to follow the specific advice given on a regular and timely basis.

Here are some of the newsletters available:

• *No-Load Investor,* P.O. Box 318, Irvington-on-Hudson, NY 10533, is edited by Sheldon Jacobs, who recommends no-load funds based on their long-term track record. When he perceives a fund's performance lagging, he recommends switching into other funds with better performance.

• *Donoghue's Moneyletter,* 290 Eliot Street, Box 91004, Ashland, MA 01721, focuses on current performance trends, as does *No Load Fund X,* 235 Montgomery St., San Francisco, CA 94104.

• *Jay Schabacker's Mutual Fund Investing,* 7811 Montrose Road, Potomac, MD 20854, also evaluates current performance, and advocates readers switching frequently from one fund to another.

• *The Mutual Fund Letter,* 680 North Lake Shore Drive, Suite 2038, Chicago, IL 60611, advises a buy-and-hold approach to investing in mutual funds. Newsletter editor Dr. Gerald Perritt focuses on the portfolio holdings of various mutual funds to be sure they match the investment objectives of the fund.

• *United Mutual Fund Selector,* 101 Prescott Street, Wellesley Hills, MA 02181, also focuses on long-term objectives rather than frequent switches.

• *Mutual Fund Forecaster* and *Income & Safety,* published by the Institute of Econometric Research, 2471 North Federal Highway, Fort Lauderdale, FL 33306, focus on mathematical analysis of past performance to forecast fund returns for the coming year. While the *Mutual Fund Forecaster* focuses on equity funds, *Income & Safety* focuses on bond funds, especially on creditworthiness and yield, and predicts which ones would fare best if interest rates changed by 1 percent.

• *Morningstar Five-Star Investor* newsletter is published by Morningstar, Inc., 225 West Wacker Drive, Chicago, IL 60606. It focuses on the fundamentals of mutual fund investing, and tracks five hundred top funds, giving you key statistics on performance, risk, operations, and other data.

• *Louis Rukeyser's Mutual Funds,* 1101 King Street, Suite 400, Alexandria, VA 22314, is a chatty publication that focuses on fund managers and offers advice from experts, much as Mr. Rukeyser's fabled TV show, *Wall Street Week,* does. Each issue of the newsletter also contains total return, sales charges, and expense ratios for the top one hundred funds in five major categories.

12
· · · · · · · ·

GROWING YOUR PORTFOLIO AS YOU MATURE

Are you looking for no-risk investments that increase in value over the years? Ponce de León searched for the fountain that would allow him to grow older without aging—but searching for investments that will provide high returns with little risk is not quite as impossible a quest. It's true that the Conserver, who invests for the short term, will always have to accept a lower return in exchange for price stability, or else run a great risk of short-term loss. However, a high average return with little risk *is* possible for the Striver, who invests long-term, because down years will be offset in the long run by good years.

Those who desire high returns with no short-term risk are like the woman who asked the butcher to cut a side of beef entirely into T-bone steaks, because that was what her family liked best. To get T-bones in your investment future, you have to accept some chuck roast and hamburger as well. If you can weather the lean years to obtain fatter returns, you will be greatly rewarded as a long-term investor. If over time you find you cannot withstand extreme investment volatility, decide what is tolerable to you. Then modify your portfolio, choosing a balance that is as close to your upper risk tolerance as possible, to maximize your portfolio returns.

Adjusting Your Portfolio as It Grows

You have created the best portfolio for you right now, but as your life changes over the years, so must your investments. Life changes in unexpected ways, and after any major shift in your circumstances, you must reassess the funds you have chosen to determine if they still suit your situation. For example, if you lost your job, are offered early retirement, have a new baby, or inherit money, all of these will affect your financial goals, which in turn affect the way you invest your money.

To decide whether it is time to readjust your goals, and thus your financial portfolio, consider these factors:

- today's economic climate and the economic outlook for the future
- your income and dependents
- your changing financial position
- your age and stage in life

Every investor is different, and as your wealth grows, your ability to withstand volatility may change. For that reason, you will want to adjust the recommended asset mixes periodically to fit your particular circumstances.

Investments with the greatest long-term growth potential bear the greatest risk for a near-term nosedive. Until you have experienced market volatility firsthand, you won't be able to know how you will react. As time passes and you mature as an investor, you will understand more about your investment style and financial temperament, and how well you tolerate market ups and downs.

Keep It Sweet and Simple

Your mutual fund portfolio can be as simple or as complex as you choose. For example, assume your ideal asset mix is 60 percent stocks and 40 percent bonds. To invest simply, you can choose a balanced fund that holds securities in that ratio. If you prefer complexity, for the equity portion of your portfolio you can invest 10 percent each in an aggressive growth fund, two growth funds, one growth and income equity fund, and two foreign stock funds (one emerging market and one international). Combine these equity investments with 10 percent each in a long-term corporate bond fund, a high-income bond fund, a corporate intermediate bond fund, and a global short-term bond fund. If taxes are a problem, you might substitute municipal bonds for the corporate bonds and choose a variable annuity for the equity investments. Or your investments could be somewhere between the simplicity and complexity of these two extremes.

Having more funds doesn't necessarily reduce your risk. At a certain point, it just complicates your life. In particular, it is foolish to have two funds that do exactly the same thing. For example, in the complex portfolio above you purchased two growth funds. Rather than invest in two that have similar styles, pick one that leans toward the value style of investing and another that leans toward the growth style—or choose two that concentrate in different areas of the economy (for example, one that has a number of technology stocks, and another that is more broadly diversified).

Trim Your Investment Sails as You Near Port

As you near your goal, be it college education for your children or retirement for yourself, it is time gradually to cut back risk. Perhaps you were aggressively investing in equities for your young child's college education. When you are within four years of your goal it is time to reduce your equities to 60 percent or so of your portfolio. The reason is clear: If you will need one-quarter of your child's education fund in four years, and one-quarter the year after that, you can't take the risk that the stock market will enter a prolonged bear phase. Fortunately, bear markets generally last only a year or two, rarely three years, so moving toward short-term bonds and cash beginning four years from your goal will ensure that your money will be available when you need it.

What We Can
Expect in the Future

Over the coming years, we will undoubtedly see many innovations in the mutual fund industry.

- *Mutual funds will become easier to buy and sell,* as we buy and sell through our home computers. Some of the on-line services are beginning to offer that option to investors.
- *You will be able to research funds through your computer.* Several of the on-line services, such as America On-Line and CompuServe, have that option available now.
- *The prospectus will be reduced to a manageable page,* rather than the baffling multipage booklet it is now. This has been suggested to the Securities and Exchange Commission, and is under consideration.
- *Mutual fund statements will become standardized and easier to read.* Many mutual fund companies now issue statements that give the entire year's history for your fund at a glance, but no real progress has been made toward standardization. However, as more and more investors enter the mutual fund market, and as competition increases, more pressure will be put upon the fund companies to provide uniform, easy-to-read information.
- *Year-end statements will give you all the information you need to prepare your tax return,* including all sales during the year, along with the tax basis of the shares sold. Many mutual fund companies are now beginning to provide that information to investors.
- *Funds will become more competitive,* and fund companies will sponsor more and more seminars for the public to educate people on the benefits of their funds and of mutual funds in general. Although mutual fund companies have provided seminars through stockbrokers for years, not many of the no-load and low-load companies that sell directly to the public have begun sponsoring public seminars.

• *To counter tax increases, innovative (and possibly intricate) tax-saving funds will emerge.* Remember the limited partnership craze of the eighties? If taxes increase and tax laws become more complex, we are likely to see complex packages of municipal bonds, growth funds, and funds that offset losses and deductions against gains in creative ways.

• *Banks and insurance companies will expand their mutual fund offerings.* Banks have begun creating their own conservative mutual funds, and we can expect them to continue, expanding into the growth funds market to compete with stockbrokers and other financial advisers. Insurance companies will likewise begin peddling their funds to the general public, just as stockbrokers do today.

• *Front-end loads will continue to shrink.* Because the public has begun to favor no-load funds, many funds sold through stockbrokers and financial advisers are eliminating front loads in favor of annual 12b-1 fees or disappearing back loads. But remember, there is no free lunch, and the long-term investor who buys a fund with no front load may end up paying more in the long run in annual 12b-1 fees.

• *More regulation in the mutual fund industry* will require more stringent and uniform disclosure of the nature and amount of all fees. Over the past few years, we have seen more requirements for disclosure, on the part of mutual fund companies as well as the stockbrokers who sell the funds. Brokerage firms are tightly policing their own brokers to be sure that the public is treated fairly.

• *More funds will become global,* as foreign markets grow and world markets blend. Already, many of the new funds coming on the market have the word "global" in their names, and many others have altered their strategy to invest some of their funds overseas, or in domestic companies who do a great deal of business overseas.

• *More investors will take social and environmental issues into account when investing.* By investing your money you are shaping the world. Investing in companies that pollute or ravage the environment encourages those activities. But if you invest in companies that are environmentally sound, and in companies that encourage advancement of women and minorities, you are helping to create a world that is better for all of us. That is the basic tenet of socially responsible investing.

Tips for the Successful Investor

You won't become wealthy overnight with mutual funds. Rarely do funds perform spectacularly, and when they do, you can be sure that they will experience some lean years sometime in the future. To make money with mutual funds, remember these rules:

1. *Begin investing as soon as you can.* Be patient, and put time on your side with compound growth. The longer your money is invested, the longer it has to grow. Because you can't predict the future, you must allocate your money among different types of funds to maximize returns under varied economic conditions.

2. *Add to your investments often, at regular intervals.* Start a program of dollar-cost averaging as soon as possible, with as much as you can afford, and increase your monthly investments whenever you can. What is the best time to invest? When you've got the money. Don't wait for stocks to hit bottom or for bond interest rates to soar. Invest early, and keep right on investing.

3. *Diversify, in accordance with your own timeline and goals.* Portfolios are a reflection of the economic times as well as of the needs and risk tolerances of the individuals who own them. When investing for the long term, invest as much in stocks as you can. Stocks offer the best long-term growth, and the best protection against inflation.

4. *Invest the money you'll need soon for stability, not growth.* Play it safe with your emergency fund, money you'll need to pay college tuition next year, and money for your summer vacation.

5. *Don't gamble with your core investments.* Options, futures, and start-up ventures are all gambles. You may want to take an occasional fling, but do so with money you can afford to lose. Recognize that such ventures are gambling and not investing.

6. *Always invest with taxes in mind.* Invest as much as you can afford in tax-deferred retirement plans. Tax-deferred growth will allow you to invest even more, because you won't have to pay money to Uncle Sam on your current earnings. Consider the tax consequences before you sell funds, and identify shares (see pages 85–86) or delay the sale if that will reduce taxes. Your assets will grow even faster if you delay paying taxes on the gains.

   7. *Don't panic in bear markets, or get cocky when you run with the bulls.* Stick to your long-range investment program for best results. Abraham Lincoln once said, "When you have got an elephant by the hind legs and he is trying to run away, it is best to let him run." The same thing is true of bears—let the bear market run its course, which is likely to be short. Otherwise, you may sell low and have to reinvest higher when you are ready to enter the market again.

   8. *When investing a lump sum, funnel it into the market over time,* unless you are certain you are in the midst of a relentless bull market, in which case it is better to invest immediately while prices are relatively low.

   9. *Think globally.* U.S. stocks account for only 40 percent of worldwide stock market investment. As the U.S. economy becomes a smaller and smaller part of growing international markets, you must invest globally to take advantage of the buying opportunities in the other 60 percent.

   10. *Don't buy without analyzing.* Take the time to compare the features and performance of "hot" funds, to make sure they fit your investment needs better than other funds available.

   11. *Don't own too many funds.* Generally, you need only three to eight funds to achieve portfolio diversification. More than that will only confuse you.

   12. *Keep your portfolio balanced.* It is important to maintain your original proportions by rebalancing regularly, but psychologically that is very difficult to do. Your natural tendency is to buy what's had hot recent performance; but rebalancing requires you to sell shares in recent hot performers. When the market plummets, it's time to buy more, not sell. When the market is reaching for the sky, you should reach for the phone and sell some shares, reallocating your money to funds that have declined. Rebalance often to your original percentages, particularly after a large market shift, downward or upward.

13. *Keep good records.* This will reduce tax-time anguish. Detailed records also help you analyze fund performance so you can make informed decisions.

14. *Seek professional help if you need it.* As loads shrink, professional advice is no longer expensive. If you are a do-it-yourselfer, consider a periodic checkup with a financial adviser to see how you are doing. Pay a load only if you need investment advice, or to gain entry into a fund that offers spectacular results.

15. *Educate yourself.* The more you know, the better you will become as an investor. Review this book periodically, and read other books and magazines on investment and money management topics.

16. *Be wise with your money.* To find money to invest, analyze your spending habits and see where you can save rather than spend.

17. *Don't try to time the market.* There are no perfect market timers who are expert at predicting the future. Sometimes market timers guess right, and sometimes they guess wrong. If you follow them, what they don't know *may hurt you.* Remember that your returns will be dismal if you miss the best days of the market, even though you managed to miss the worst ones as well.

18. *Pay attention to costs as well as performance.* In a down year, low costs may reduce stunning losses to more acceptable mediocre returns. Consider index funds for low-cost stock and bond investments. Although by definition these funds won't outperform the market, few funds consistently outperform the market anyway.

19. *Don't overmanage your portfolio.* Even the best funds can have slumps as well as booms. If you switch funds frequently, you may dump the steak from the frying pan into the fire and miss the sizzle altogether. Be a buy-and-hold, not a cut-and-run investor. Also, don't jump from fund to fund to pick up last year's hot performer. Chances are it won't perform nearly as well this year, and you will have dumped a well-chosen fund for a whim that didn't pan out. Chasing performance rarely pays off.

20. *Don't expect your mutual fund decisions to be right all the time.*

Some of your funds will underperform your expectations, but others will outperform your expectations. As you rebalance and weed out consistent underperformers over the years, you will achieve the overall investment return you had expected. Review your allocation strategy every few years to make sure it accurately reflects your current goals.

Keep Investing

A wag once said, "Save a little money each month, and at the end of the year you'll be surprised at how little you have." But if you keep right on saving, and invest those savings for long-term results, after a few years the growth of your little nest egg will astound you. Keep on adding to your investments, and rebalance periodically. Sophie Tucker, the famous singer, said the secret to longevity is to keep breathing; similarly, the secret to financial success is to keep investing.

Economists are famous for their predictions. Unfortunately, they almost never agree with one another at any particular time. Thomas Edison once said, "We don't know a millionth of one percent about anything," and when it comes to the future, we know even less. The true trick to making money in any economic climate is to invest and keep on investing. As you build your portfolio year after year, the market will rise and fall, as do the tides, but your portfolio will grow and grow.

As Will Rogers cautioned, "Even if you're on the right track, you'll get run over if you just sit there." Get on the right track, and keep adding to your portfolio, monitoring and rebalancing as needed, and you'll profit in any economy. Give your investments the gift of time, and you will be rewarded with a lifetime of financial security.

INDEX